July 1989

To Mom + Dad,

Thanks for a great adventure.
I knew the wild animals were your
favorite part of Africa.

Love
Ted

The Kruger

A Supreme African Wilderness

To Linda and Cecil

AN AFROPIX EDITION

Afropix Publishers
Wellington House
17 Union Street
Jersey

© Bruce Aiken 1988

ISBN 0 409 10605 4

Distributed in South Africa by

 **Butterworths**
Professional Publishers (Pty) Ltd
Reg No 87/03997/07

DURBAN
JOHANNESBURG
PRETORIA
CAPE TOWN

Printed by Interpak, Pietermaritzburg
The imprint Butterworths is used under licence

Contents

Pages 2 & 3: Sunrise over the Lebombo Mountains. (Tshokwane)

Author's note

It was with considerable apprehension that I drove through the Paul Kruger gate en route to the park's headquarters some four years ago. Ahead of me lay the task of producing a documentary book on one of the world's most famous national parks.

From the beginning my aim was to photograph as much of the park as possible, including some of the spectacular remote areas. After all, the Kruger National Park is not only the heritage of all South Africans but of wildlife lovers everywhere.

This heritage is becoming more valuable every day as the pace of African wildlife destruction continues to accelerate. Soon the Kruger will be one of the continent's last great wildernesses.

My first task was to undertake a comprehensive orientation tour, so as to decide how much time should be allocated to photography in each area.

It was during this tour that I realized for the first time how vast a territory had to be covered. Previously, I had photographed in parks where there were few roads and hardly any facilities for tourists, and where limited dry-season water sources dictated the movements of game. Photography was confined mainly to a few well-known locations.

The tour lasted one and a half months. Altogether, I covered over 4 000 km of the more than 6 000 km road network. I learned that there are 17 well-equipped camps to accommodate the approximately half a million wildlife enthusiasts who visit the park each year, and that Skukuza is larger than many of the towns in the Lowveld. Even more of a surprise was the abundance of water. Seven major rivers traverse the park from west to east. These are the Crocodile, Sabie, Olifants, Letaba, Shingwidzi, Luvuvhu and Limpopo rivers. There are also numerous streams, many of which hold water during the dry season; more than 300 water-holes serviced by windmills; and various man-made dams. The game is therefore spread throughout the park, and the importance of dry-season concentrations for photography is minimized.

For management purposes, the park is divided into 22 sections. The average area of these sections is a massive 900 km², and each is controlled by a game ranger and his staff. When I entered a section, my first call was always on the game ranger. I felt privileged to be able to consult the rangers, and quickly learned the value of their advice.

The knowledge and impressions gained on the tour are the foundations of this book. Perhaps what impressed me most was the variety of scenery and wildlife. Whether it is mountainous terrain, great rivers, thick bush, open plains, mopane veld, sandstone communities or magnificent forests, the Kruger has it all. Consequently, the park is unequalled in Southern Africa for the variety of its wildlife.

I calculated that the photography would take me three years. Shortly before I began, the National Parks Board informed me that, as certain scientific projects had come to an end, I could have access to several collared lions in the southern central district. As the collars contained tiny transmitters, it would be possible to home in on the lions at any time. This was too good an opportunity to miss, as it would enable me quickly to complete the lion photography for the book. What we had not anticipated was that two of the collared lionesses would turn out to be members of a massive pride of 39. Inevitably, I and my assistant Debbie Fair became totally engrossed with the pride, and spent more than 1 000 hours following them at night, sharing and recording their adventures, and witnessing 57 kills. The result was the book NIGHTSTALK – THE STORY OF A KRUGER PRIDE.

A year later than planned, with many fond memories of our lions, we started the general photography for this book. During the next three years we visited many fascinating areas and our time in the park came to an end all to soon.

I was indeed fortunate to obtain interviews for this book with Johan Kloppers, the head of wildlife management in the park, and Dave Chapman, the park's most experienced trail ranger. I have no hesitation in saying that their straightforward and often philosophical answers to my questions will be of great interest to wildlife enthusiasts.

For the sake of continuity and easy reference, I have divided the main photographic part of the book into four sections: the mixed vegetation and terrain of the southern part of the park; the rolling grassy plains of the southern central district; the mopane veld of the northern central district; and the sandveld communities and lush riverine forests of the north.

The introductory text to each of these sections contains a description of each camp and the surrounding area; indicates what animals are most commonly seen there; and suggests routes for game drives. I have kept the text short but comprehensive so that it can be used as an easy reference guide.

During our years in the park we found that certain roads offered consistently good game-viewing. These are recommended as routes for game drives. Where photographs taken from well-known roads are scenically representative I have indicated their location at the end of the relevant caption.

Left: Crocodiles sun themselves on sandy beaches, and red flame creepers add a dash of colour to tropical forests, as the Luvuvhu River emerges from the gorges at the foot of the Maschicindudzi hills.

How it all began

The early history of the Kruger National Park is closely connected with the lives of its great pioneering figures, and with events that were shaping South African history as far back as the beginning of the nineteenth century.

In 1806, after almost a century and a half of Dutch rule, the British secured possession of the Cape Colony. British colonists were settled in the eastern region, and provision was made for English to replace Dutch as the official language. Resentment of British policies and a wish for independence soon prompted the Great Trek of 1835-37, during which thousands of Boers trekked northwards to find new lands.

Two main routes were taken by the Trekkers. Many journeyed north-eastwards to Natal. Others considered the threat of British annexation of this territory too great and made their way northwards across the Orange River. Most of the latter settled in what are now the Orange Free State and the Transvaal.

At that time the Transvaal Lowveld, especially what is now the Kruger National Park, was a vast expanse of inhospitable bushveld. The area was inhabited by hostile tribes and was rife with malaria and sleeping sickness. Nevertheless, finding a route through this wilderness was imperative if the Boers were to obtain access to the Indian Ocean and cut their dependence on the Cape Colony for supplies.

The first major expeditions to attempt to cross the Lowveld proved disastrous. Van Rensburg and his party were massacred by tribesmen at Columbine, some 80 kilometres north of the confluence of the Limpopo and Olifants Rivers. Two years later, in 1838, Louis Trichardt's expedition reached Lourenço Marques (now Maputo), but suffered considerable loss of life through malaria. For the time being, it was decided to halt all further attempts to find a route to the sea.

In those days Lourenço Marques was a small settlement established by the Portuguese to mark their claim to the region. One of the town's colourful inhabitants was João Albasini, a tough Portuguese national of Italian birth who had made a name for himself as a trader and an elephant hunter. Albasini first became aware of the influx of Boers into the Transvaal when he met Louis Trichardt after the latter's fateful journey. Six years later Albasini was again in Lourenço Marques when Hendrik Potgieter's expedition reached the town. Seeing an opportunity for trade, Albasini soon established a trade route across the dreaded 'fly belt', using African porters to carry goods to a post north of today's Pretoriuskop rest camp. The Boers came down from the escarpment, purchased goods from Albasini, and then returned without risk of traversing the 'fly belt' to the east. The opening of this route to Delagoa Bay was to have great significance for the Lowveld and its wildlife in the years to come.

Boer settlement north of the Orange River continued to prosper and in 1852, in terms of the Sand River Convention, the British government recognized the independence of the Transvaal, this paving the way for the establishment of the South African Republic in 1856. Pretoria became the capital. The Orange Free State had become a republic a year earlier.

For almost two decades the Boer republics enjoyed a period free from outside interference. Then, in 1870, the first large gold strike was made at Lydenburg. A year later there was another at Mac-Mac on the Great Escarpment, followed by others at Lydenburg and Pilgrim's Rest, and the largest in 1884 near Barberton. Following the gold came the multitudes, and the trade route to Delagoa Bay assumed a new significance as transport riders, such as Sir Percy Fitz-Patrick of 'Jock of the Bushveld' fame, carried mining equipment and other goods from Lourenço Marques to the mines by ox-wagon. The route soon became a road and made access to the Lowveld's wildlife much easier. Once all the game in the vicinity of the towns and mines had been slaughtered, professional hunters ventured further and further into the Lowveld in their efforts to supply the mining communities with meat, and to hunt elephants for their ivory. The region's formerly prolific wildlife was rapidly being exterminated.

The new-found mineral wealth of the South African Republic elicited a new phase of colonial interest in the region and in 1877 the British annexed the Republic. The Boers, led by Paul Kruger protested vigorously, but to no avail. Then, in 1880, the Boers defiantly reproclaimed their republic and defeated a British force in the ensuing battles of Laing's Nek and Majuba Hill. Unwilling to contest the Boers' wish for freedom any further at that stage, the British concluded the Treaty of Pretoria on 5 April 1881, as a result of which the South African Republic was again given independence, but under British suzerainty.

Left: In 1902 Colonel Stevenson-Hamilton, often referred to as the 'father of the Kruger', was appointed head ranger of the Sabie Game Reserve. For the next forty-four years he was to guide the destiny of this famous piece of Africa.

Overleaf: Wildebeest welcome in a mist-covered dawn.

Fortunately for the Lowveld's wildlife, the gold boom of the eastern Transvaal lasted only a few more years and was replaced by the more famous Witwatersrand strikes. The first rich Witwatersrand reef was opened in 1886, and Johannesburg quickly grew to accommodate the mining communities.

In 1883 Paul Kruger was elected president of the South African Republic. For the next sixteen years, until the outbreak of the Anglo-Boer war in 1899, he was to lead his people through one of the most difficult periods in their struggle for independence. During this time he reached a position of prominence among an electorate that few politicians have achieved. He became a father figure to the Boer nation and, many years after his death, reverence for this great man may have decided the vote in favour of the proclamation of a national park named in his honour.

Paul Kruger was the first politician to realize the urgent need for conservation in the South African Republic. A man of great vision, he feared that no game would be left for future generations. Accordingly, in his first term as president, he made a strong plea for areas to be set aside where nature could remain unspoilt 'as the Creator made it'. At first, most members of the volksraad found his views unacceptable – almost scandalous. It had always been assumed that game belonged to everyone and had always been there to shoot. Year after year the fate of the dwindling game population in the Transvaal was debated in the volksraad.

In 1889, President Kruger proposed establishing two specific areas for game preservation: an area in the Soutpansberg district (the present Shingwedzi), and the Pongola area between Swaziland and Zululand. After much opposition from certain members of the volksraad, the Pongola reserve was proclaimed on 13 June 1894.

One of the president's most ardent supporters for the idea of a game reserve in the Lowveld was Mr R K Loveday, the sitting member for Barberton, who played an important role in conservation in the years to come. On 6 September 1895, Mr van Wyk, the volksraad member for Krugersdorp supported by Mr Loveday, submitted the following motion:

The undersigned, seeing that nearly all big game in this Republic have been exterminated, and that those animals still remaining are becoming less day by day, so that there is a danger of their becoming altogether extinct in the near future, request to be permitted . . . to depart from the order paper to discuss the desirability of authorising the Government to proclaim as a Government Game Reserve where killing of game shall altogether be prohibited, certain portions of the district of Lydenburg, being Government land, where most of the big game species are still

to be found, to wit, the territory situated between the Crocodile and the Sabie Rivers with boundaries as follows . . .

The motion was debated and passed by the volksraad on September 17. Finally, on 26 March 1898, a notice appeared in the Gazette officially proclaiming the Sabie Game Reserve.

But the time was not ripe for establishing a game reserve, as matters were coming to a head between the Boers and the British. The Boers wanted independence, while the British were determined to incorporate the Boer republics in a South African federation under the British flag. Eventually, on 13 October 1899, war broke out.

It was a hard and bitter war, with early victories on both sides. Inevitably, however, the considerable numerical advantages enjoyed by the British forces turned the tide against the gallant Boer commandos. Eleven months after the outbreak of war, on 1 September 1900, Lord Roberts was able to issue a proclamation annexing the Transvaal. By then the last pitched battle of the war had been fought at Berg-en-Dal near Belfast, and the Boers had lost both their capitals. The Boer commandos and government then took to the field, and the famous 'war of movement' began. President Kruger, being too old to ride with the commandos, was sent to Europe to promote the cause of his people. He died in exile in Switzerland a few years later.

For the already seriously depleted wildlife of the Lowveld the war was a disaster. British troops regularly shot to supplement their rations and Boer commandos became increasingly dependent on wildlife for food. The black tribes, finding that there was no control over their hunting, also exacted a heavy toll. Fortunately, in the midst of this killing, there were some noteworthy champions of conservation. One was Major Greenhill-Gardyne, the adjutant of Steinaecker's Horse, which was stationed at Komatipoort. Major Greenhill-Gardyne did much to curb the unnecessary killing of game by his men and by local tribesmen. He also wrote a report proposing conservation measures for the Sabie Game Reserve. Many of these measures were adopted after the war.

Another conservationist whose ideas were noted by the post-war government, was the well-known naturalist and sportsman, Abel Chapman. Shortly before the outbreak of war, while on a hunting trip north of the Sabie River, he was struck by the potential of the region for a game reserve. He set about collecting data and in 1900 drew up a detailed report proposing that the entire area between the Crocodile and Limpopo Rivers, and the Lebombo and Drakensberg Mountains, be made one large game reserve. (These boundaries were very similar to those adopted in 1903.)

On 31 May 1902, peace was declared. By the Treaty of

Vereeniging, the Boers accepted British sovereignty but were promised representative institutions as soon as circumstances permitted.

Some time before the end of the war RK Loveday had started negotiations for the reproclamation of the Sabie Game Reserve. Influenced by Loveday, and by Greenhill-Gardyne's and Chapman's reports, Lord Milner reproclaimed the reserve shortly after peace had been declared.

It was at this stage that Stevenson-Hamilton, often referred to as 'the father of the Kruger', began his association with the Sabie Game Reserve. For the next forty-four years he was to guide the destiny of this famous piece of Africa.

James Stevenson-Hamilton was born in Dublin on 2 October 1867. His mother was heiress of the estates of Fairholm and Kirkton in Lanarkshire, Scotland, and his father a captain in the 12th Royal Lancers. As he was a member of the privileged upper class, his future seemed assured. His parents had probably foreseen a military career for him and an early retirement on the estates he would inherit. They could not have anticipated that he was to spend most of his adult life in Africa, campaigning for and establishing his 'Cinderella' (his own term for the Kruger Park).

When still a young boy, Stevenson-Hamilton inherited his mother's estates. His early years followed the course expected. He went to school at Rugby, and then went on to Sandhurst to prepare for a military career. In March 1888 he was given his first commission in the 6th (Inniskilling) Dragoons and sailed to Natal to join his regiment, where he fought against the Zulus. In 1890, he returned to Britain to the glamorous life of a young cavalry officer. But he had not forgotten Africa and in 1898 he obtained a year's leave from his regiment to accompany Major Gibbons's expedition to Barotseland (now western Zambia), where he explored and hunted. During his absence he was promoted to captain and was also made deputy lieutenant of Lanarkshire.

For the first part of the Anglo-Boer War, Stevenson-Hamilton commanded a small force of scouts attached to General Clements's column. After this, he served with his own regiment until the end of the war, attaining the rank of major.

Shortly after the cessation of hostilities, Stevenson-Hamilton happened to be in Johannesburg, where he met the newly appointed commissioner for native affairs, Sir Godfrey Lagden. Sir Godfrey was looking for someone suitably qualified for the post of head ranger of the newly reproclaimed Sabie Game Reserve, and the idea appealed to Stevenson-Hamilton. He was given the position on the strength of his previous hunting and exploring experience, and seconded from his regiment for two years. Although Stevenson-Hamilton looked forward to the opportunities he would have for studying wildlife, he viewed the appointment as temporary, having made the army his career.

Never having been to the Lowveld, Stevenson-Hamilton gathered what information he could about the area and then went to the Rand Club to have a look at a large map. He found the position of the Sabie Game Reserve marked as a blank space, crossed only by a few dotted lines indicating unsurveyed watercourses. Further inquiries confirmed that no one knew much about the area except the Boers, and they hunted there only during the three safe months. For the rest of the year it was considered a 'white man's grave' because of malaria.

Undaunted, Stevenson-Hamilton went to Lydenburg to be fitted out with government transport. This included a light wagon drawn by six emaciated oxen and three unsalted ponies (ponies which were not immune to horse sickness). He had the services of a general factotum called Nicholas, and a Basuto youth as a horse attendant. In addition there was a driver and a leader for the wagon and, finally, 'Toothless Jack', whose sole asset was that he could converse with the local tribesmen.

From Lydenburg, Stevenson-Hamilton took the old wagon trail down the escarpment and, at the end of a long day's trek, pulled up at the Sanderson farmhouse to find that the owner was away on a hunting trip. Sanderson, a Scotsman in his mid-fifties, was much respected throughout the Lowveld, and was one of the first professional hunters to have operated there.

The next day, leaving his wagon at Sanderson's, Stevenson-Hamilton set out on horseback to find out what he could about local conditions. His first stop was at Nelspruit, about forty-two kilometres distant. In those days, the town consisted of two corrugated iron buildings, a so-called hotel and a store. He was told that no one knew the game reserve better than Harry Wolhuter, who was probably at Komatipoort.

On reaching Komatipoort, Stevenson-Hamilton was disappointed at not finding Wolhuter, but he did meet Major Greenhill-Gardyne. After a brief visit, he returned to the Sanderson farm to collect his wagon. Sanderson had returned, and he told Stevenson-Hamilton of the herds of eland and other antelope that had covered the hills in the White River area in the seventies, and how the Lowveld had been a hunter's paradise, even though elephant and rhino had disappeared by that time. Buffalo had been the most profitable game to hunt, and had been numerous in the fly country.

On 6 August 1902, Stevenson-Hamilton set out by wagon for the game reserve. He travelled eastwards along Sanderson's recent wagon tracks, anxious for his first sight of game — especially big game. But he was to be sadly disappointed. For three days he saw no evidence that larger animals had ever existed there. On the fourth day he came across zebra, waterbuck and impala spoor and, on the fifth, actually saw a few scattered antelope. Hardly a promising beginning!

After reaching the Selati railway line, Stevenson-Hamilton turned south towards Komatipoort. On the way, the weekly train from Komatipoort to Sabie Bridge passed the wagon, which was partially concealed in thick bush. Several of the passengers, mistaking it for game, opened fire but fortunately missed — a good indication of the state of affairs in the so-called game reserve.

That evening Stevenson-Hamilton reached Gomondwane, one of the posts of Steinaecker's Horse, some eleven kilometres north of the Crocodile River. He was hospitably received and told that the officer in charge, Captain Gaza Gray, had established himself at Lower Sabie, about twelve miles to the north-east.

On his recent trip to Komatipoort, Stevenson-Hamilton had been told by Major Greenhill-Gardyne to seek out Captain Gray, because the latter was the best man to advise him on local conditions. Gray, a tough fifty, had spent many years in the Lowveld and Portuguese East Africa as a labour recruiter, and could speak the local dialects fluently. He advised Stevenson-Hamilton that there was still a fair amount of game along the Lebombos, but that it would not last much longer as it was being rapidly depleted by the tribes who lived there.

As a result of his talks with Gray, Stevenson-Hamilton made up his mind that all the tribes from the eastern and southern areas would have to be moved back to where they had come from. He also decided to divide the game reserve into districts, each under a white official with his own force of black police. In fact, much the same system as is in operation in the Kruger National Park today.

Gray agreed that, in return for being allowed to remain where he was and to graze his cattle in the reserve, he would act as an honorary ranger. His territory would be the reserve to the east of the Selati railway line between the Crocodile and Sabie Rivers. He would engage black police and generally make known the new state of affairs regarding game preservation. He stipulated that should more attractive employment come his way, he was to be free to accept it. He also offered Stevenson-Hamilton the temporary use of a corrugated-iron cottage that he owned on the banks of the Crocodile River about seven miles north of Komatipoort.

This was to be park headquarters until something more suitable could be found.

Stevenson-Hamilton then headed for Komatipoort, hoping to find Wolhuter, who had enlisted with Steinaecker's Horse. Martial law still existed at the time and, although all the other units had been disbanded, it looked as if Steinaecker's Horse might remain at Komatipoort in order to keep an armed presence in the area.

Major Greenhill-Gardyne arranged an interview between Stevenson-Hamilton and Wolhuter who had just returned from a spell of duty at the Olifants River. Stevenson-Hamilton wrote of Wolhuter:

At that time Harry Christopher Wolhuter, for so many years to be associated with me in the development and administration of the Sabie Game Reserve, was about twenty-seven years old. Tall and spare, with a heavy black moustache, a man of quiet determined manner and few words, he looked exactly what he was, a typical farmer, bushman, and hunter of the best type.

After initial hesitation, Wolhuter decided to accept the position Stevenson-Hamilton had offered him. In his book, 'Memories of a Game Ranger', Wolhuter wrote:

After turning the pros and cons well over in my mind, my natural love of the life won the issue, so when I met Major Stevenson-Hamilton again on the appointed day it was to accept his offer of employment as a game ranger in the Sabie Reserve (as it was then called). That was forty-five years ago, and I have never regretted my decision. I would like to say at this point, that one could have had no better chief than Colonel J. Stevenson-Hamilton. I look back upon my long and very interesting, association with him with undimmed pleasure; no superior officer was more loyal, kindly and considerate to his subordinates.

Wolhuter resigned from Steinaecker's Horse and was allowed to choose the section of the reserve which would come under his control. As he had spent most of his earlier life in the Pretoriuskop area and it was relatively free of malaria, he chose it as his territory.

Stevenson-Hamilton then embarked on his first major tour of his domain. He borrowed two pack mules from Steinaecker's Horse, and set out in an easterly direction past Ship Mountain, and then turned northwards to the Sabie River. Game was scarce and, apart from a few wildebeest and a couple of warthog, he saw little. It was not until he had neared Sabie Bridge (now Skukuza) that he saw waterbuck and impala in any numbers.

It was on this trip that Stevenson-Hamilton was to taste adventure in the game reserve for the first time. One night, shortly after retiring, he was awakened by frantic shouting and the growls of a lion. Hastily grabbing his rifle, he rushed

Above: The four musketeers.

out of the tent to find 'Toothless Jack' excitedly yelling and hurling burning logs into the darkness. There was little Stevenson-Hamilton could do, but he fired a few shots in the direction of the growls in the hope of discouraging the lion, which was presumably after the mules. Fortunately, one of the blacks managed to calm the animals and prevent them from running off into the claws of the waiting predator.

Once everything had calmed down, 'Toothless Jack' described what had happened. Just before going to sleep, he had sat up to put another log on the fire. As the flames brightened, they illuminated a huge male lion standing about three metres away, watching him. At that moment the mules began to panic and, with commendable bravery, the old black attendant had hurled a blazing log at the lion, which then withdrew into the darkness. After this experience, Stevenson-Hamilton was careful never to travel in lion country without dogs, and always to build a thorn enclosure round his camp.

The tour was completed about a fortnight later, and the following few months were devoted to learning the topography of the reserve.

Stevenson-Hamilton next turned his attention to the territory north of the Sabie River. In many ways it was a better game area than the Sabie Reserve. In his opinion, and that of many of the more prominent Lowveld residents, the area should be added to the reserve. Unfortunately, about half the several hundred large farms into which the area had been divided were privately owned.

During a strenuous fortnight in Pretoria Stevenson-Hamilton called separately on the managers of all the large land-owning companies. He was remarkably successful. Virtually every one of them agreed to his proposals. They would hand over control of their farms for a period of five years; in return, the reserve's staff were to protect the flora and fauna, prevent prospecting, and collect native rents.

Armed with the landowners' permission, Stevenson-Hamilton approached Sir Godfrey Lagden and induced him to adopt the plan. Ten months later the addition was gazetted.

During his trip, Stevenson-Hamilton also initiated the drafting of a set of regulations to be put to the legislative council as soon as possible. Steps were also taken to confer judicial powers on the warden of the reserve as, without such powers, cases involving poachers and other offenders had to be sent to Barberton or Lydenburg for trial. Sometimes this involved as much as a two-weeks absence for the police escort and the witnesses. The new regulations were also designed to confer on staff members powers of arrest and detention for matters within the reserve.

Stevenson-Hamilton was also successful in getting the western boundary of the reserve redefined. By extending the reserve another seventeen kilometres to the west, to the foot of the Drakensberg, he secured valuable land suitable for game such as kudu, reedbuck, sable and oribi.

On returning from Pretoria, Stevenson-Hamilton moved his headquarters to Sabie Bridge. He used the old blockhouse of Steinaecker's Horse as his dining room and general living quarters and slept in a hut made of boiler plates. This was accommodation far superior to the rat-infested corrugated-iron cottage at Crocodile Bridge.

Stevenson-Hamilton next turned his attention to restoring the wildlife stocks. He had noted that there were proportionately more lion than normal in relation to the number of antelope. This was because lions were rarely shot as their skins had little value. He decided that one way of encouraging the development of antelope stocks was to introduce the culling of predators (this with due regard to the continued existence of all species).

Shortly before his trip to Pretoria, he had engaged a ranger for the Crocodile Bridge area. After two months' service, the man left and Stevenson-Hamilton was fortunate to secure Thomas Duke for the post. Duke was about forty years old and, when still a child, had emigrated from Ireland to South Africa with his parents. For the last year of the war Stevenson-Hamilton had served with him in Rimington's Column, and had been so impressed by his abilities, particularly as a linguist, that he had been determined to secure his services for the game reserve. Because of Duke's proficiency in the Xhosa language, the Africans called him 'M'Xosa'. Some of these nicknames were not so complimentary. One man Stevenson-Hamilton knew was under the impression that his African name was 'The Great Elephant' (a very complimentary term). In actual fact he was referred to as 'Hyaena Face'. Stevenson-Hamilton learned that his own nickname was 'Skukuza', which meant 'He who sweeps clean.'

Shortly after Duke had been appointed the ranger at Crocodile Bridge, Gray resigned as honorary ranger at Lower Sabie to take up a position with the Witwatersrand Native Labour Association, and Stevenson-Hamilton transferred Duke to take over his duties.

Stevenson-Hamilton then secured the services of R C de Laporte as a ranger. De Laporte had been the lieutenant in charge of intelligence in Rimington's Column. He was about twenty-eight, able and tactful — very necessary qualities for controlling the Crocodile River section, which he then took over.

In August 1903 various events focused public attention on the new reserve. A party of senior officers of the South African Constabulary had trekked down through the reserve with transport oxen from the Olifants River, and from Komatipoort had entered Portuguese East Africa. Apparently they intended re-entering the reserve just south of the Olifants River, choosing to ignore the risk of spreading the East Coast fever which was rife at the time.

Feeling that there must be an explanation, Stevenson-Hamilton sent Wolhuter to the Olifants to intercept them. Unfortunately, Wolhuter had to return for a second horse, as his first had succumbed to horse sickness. Meanwhile, the party had returned to the Transvaal, and the natives reported that they had shot several animals in a protected area, and that their oxen had been dying from East Coast fever.

Wolhuter made a second start with the intention of obtaining enough evidence to establish if the reports were true. On returning from a patrol, he decided to push on ahead of his blacks to a water-hole where he would meet them later. Just as it was getting too dark to see, his horse was attacked by two lions. Wolhuter fell to the ground almost on top of the one lion, which grabbed him by his right shoulder. The other lion raced after the horse, followed by Wolhuter's dog, Bull. After being dragged for about fifty metres, Wolhuter succeeded in stabbing the lion three times with a sheath knife he always carried in his belt. The lion slunk off into the darkness, and some time later he heard its death rattle.

Realizing that the second lion would probably not catch the horse and would return, Wolhuter climbed a small tree, all the time growing weaker from loss of blood. The second lion returned shortly after Wolhuter had settled in a fork about four metres from the ground, and seemed about to climb the tree when Bull appeared on the scene. For the next hour, until the blacks arrived, Bull managed to keep the lion at bay by rushing at it and barking.

It was four days before Wolhuter's wounds received any sort of dressing. The first Stevenson-Hamilton heard of the incident was when, one evening, Wolhuter's policemen appeared at Sabie Bridge leading his horse. They told him the gist of what had happened and said that Wolhuter was now in Barberton hospital.

Later, Stevenson-Hamilton and Sir Alfred Pease, the magistrate at Barberton, sent a jointly-signed account of the incident to the *Field*. The story was taken up by newspapers all round the world, Wolhuter became famous, and many people were made aware of the reserve for the first time.

With Wolhuter as a casualty, Stevenson-Hamilton sent de Laporte to the Olifants. He gathered sufficient evidence for the officers of the constabulary to be charged. In the ensuing court case one of the accused was found guilty of having shot a wildebeest, and fined £5. The fact that Stevenson-Hamilton had dared to charge these high officials and that he had secured a conviction was not popular with the local police. Nevertheless, respect for law enforcement in the Sabie Game Reserve increased considerably.

Meanwhile, the regulations that Stevenson-Hamilton had drafted had been proclaimed, as had the Shingwedzi Game Reserve and the addition to the Sabie Game Reserve. He then set out to tour the Shingwedzi district.

In the three hundred kilometres covered, he saw a total of nine kudu, five waterbuck, three tsessebe, and perhaps a dozen duiker. He noticed the spoor of two giraffe and on one occasion caught a fleeting glimpse of a lion. The game had virtually been wiped out.

Shortly after the war the government had reproclaimed the Pongola Reserve, which was a strip of seven farms lying below the Lebombo Mountains and forming a narrow wedge between Zululand and Swaziland. The reserve had been placed under Stevenson-Hamilton's control and Windham, the secretary of the native affairs department, had recommended a Major Fraser as the ranger of the reserve.

Fraser arrived from Scotland and spent a few weeks with Stevenson-Hamilton in mid-1903 before taking up his duties. He was well over six feet tall, very broad, and in his late forties. He had had considerable experience of Indian shikar, and was quick to adapt to local conditions.

After completing the Shingwedzi tour, Stevenson-Hamilton journeyed to the Pongola Reserve to inspect the last of his domains. It soon became evident to him that the area held little potential and he transferred Fraser to the Shingwedzi Game Reserve, where he was stationed at a place called 'Malunzane' on the Tsende River.

As Stevenson-Hamilton had by now been given the judicial functions of a justice of the peace, he was provided with a public prosecutor and clerk of the court. He was G R Healy, a very junior corporal of the South African Constabulary. Healy was about twenty-one years of age and had come to South Africa as a second lieutenant in an Irish militia regiment. He was a tall, loose-limbed youth, and people were apt to try and take advantage of him – to their subsequent regret.

Stevenson-Hamilton's two-year secondment from his regiment was almost at an end. He had been so involved with establishing the game reserve, that he had not been aware of the antagonism that certain Lowveld residents felt towards him. Many resented the fact that they had not been allowed to help officials to cull predators, and some felt that the post of warden should not have been given to a foreigner. Stevenson-Hamilton was also unpopular with the constabulary after his successful prosecution of one of their high-ranking officers.

East Coast fever was widespread at the time and, as a counter-measure, cattle had been confined to the farms they were on. As the Sabie Game Reserve had been surveyed as more than one farm, Stevenson-Hamilton was restricted in the use of his ox-wagon – a necessary method of transport for him. Even though his oxen had had no contact with other oxen, he could not risk using his wagon as the local police made frequent visits to the reserve, hoping to find that he

had broken some regulation. He found a way round this by persuading the authorities in Pretoria to regard the Sabie Reserve as one farm. He also introduced restrictions denying domestic animals entry to the reserve, and the Sabie and Shingwedzi reserves were almost the only two areas in the Transvaal which escaped the disease.

All too soon Stevenson-Hamilton's first term was over, and with it ended the two most outstanding years in the history of conservation in South Africa. In this short time Stevenson-Hamilton and his hand-picked team of game rangers had established effective control over an area larger than the present Kruger National Park. All that was necessary to achieve the permanent proclamation of the entire area as one large game reserve or national park was for the government to buy out the private landowners. This was not an insurmountable obstacle, as their farms were only virgin bush with relatively low farming potential.

The War Office cabled Stevenson-Hamilton to return to Britain and his regiment, and he found himself torn between two worlds. On the one hand, there was the prospect of a distinguished military career and time to enjoy his estates in Lanarkshire; on the other, his 'Cinderella'.

June 1905 found Stevenson-Hamilton back in the Sabie Game Reserve. A few months earlier, conservation had lost a powerful ally when Lord Milner had left South Africa, to be succeeded by Lord Selborne. The reserves were taken over by the colonial secretary, Mr Patrick Duncan, and his assistant, Mr Moor. The latter's attitude towards Stevenson-Hamilton and his work was one of amused tolerance.

On the political front, a number of changes were taking place. The Liberals were returned to power in Britain in January 1906. They believed that the best way to maintain control over South Africa was to grant self-government to the former republics, by way of general elections.

In February 1907, a general election in the Transvaal resulted in victory for the Het Volk party. Louis Botha became prime minister, and General Smuts the colonial secretary. The game reserves were in Smuts' portfolio.

Shortly after Stevenson-Hamilton's return from Britain, he was sitting in Hannemann's Hotel at Komatipoort when Hanneman remarked, 'When is this reserve of yours going to be thrown open for shooting?' Stevenson-Hamilton replied that he hoped never. 'What!' exclaimed Hanneman. 'Do you mean to tell me that the government is going to spend thousands of pounds every year just to keep game? What is the use of it, anyhow?'

Overleaf: The view from the Stevenson-Hamilton memorial. (S22 south of Skukuza).

17

Rather taken aback, Stevenson-Hamilton realized that he had no firm objective as to how the game reserve should be used. In London he had heard about the great success of the American national parks, and he sent off for all the available literature. He wondered whether the South African public would ever change its attitude of wanting to shoot wildlife, and be prepared to pay to view it. He always looked back on that day in Hannemann's Hotel as the first time that he began to visualize the Kruger National Park as we know it. Meanwhile, other developments were taking place which were to influence the history of the park.

In 1909 a decision was made to continue building the Selati railway line. Construction had begun in the early 1890s, the objective being to link Komatipoort with the Selati goldfields, but this had been discontinued because of the bankruptcy of the contracting company. Sabie Bridge was to have a proper railway bridge and the line was to cut through Stevenson-Hamilton's dining room. By 1912 the railway had reached Tzaneen.

On 31 May 1910, after being passed by the Lords and the Commons, and being signed by King Edward VII, the South Africa Act came into effect. The four colonies were to become provinces of the Union of South Africa with the names 'Cape of Good Hope', 'Natal', 'Transvaal', and the 'Orange Free State'. Executive power was to be vested in the king and was to be administered on his behalf by a governor-general appointed by the Crown for five years, and a cabinet of not more than ten members. Gladstone became governor-general, Louis Botha, prime minister; and Smuts, minister of the interior, mines and defence.

Stevenson-Hamilton had hoped that, with the coming of Union, the game reserves would be placed under one central governing body, so that they would be less susceptible to local influences. This wish was not realized and, together with the general wildlife preservation of the province, the reserves were placed under the Transvaal administration, headed by Mr Johann Rissik.

On one of his visits to Pretoria, Stevenson-Hamilton was sent for by Mr Rissik. Rissik sat with a map of the Sabie Game Reserve spread in front of him, and informed Stevenson-Hamilton that pressure had been placed on him to allow the grazing of sheep in the south-western part of the reserve. All Stevenson-Hamilton could do was to persuade Rissik to introduce a grazing fee and restrictions on shooting.

Other clouds loomed on the horizon. The agreement with the land companies was coming up for its third term of renewal, and certain of the farmers were not disposed to continue the arrangement. The South African Railways also began pressing for the establishment of a strip of land on either side of the railway line, to be occupied by farmers, as this would bring considerable benefit to goods traffic.

In August 1914 World War I broke out and Stevenson-Hamilton enlisted. De Laporte agreed to take over as warden, but promised to stay for only as long as his conscience would allow him. Healy had already departed overseas, and the staff was reduced to Wolhuter, Fraser and Duke. Wolhuter, still suffering from the effects of his mauling by the lion, was rejected for military service on medical grounds; the other two were too old to enlist. Fraser took over the wardenship from de Laporte in 1917, and a man named Streeter, an old Lowvelder, was temporarily appointed to the Shingwedzi Reserve in his absence.

During 1915 hostility towards the Sabie Game Reserve reached a new peak. Following a motion in the Transvaal Provincial Council from Mr S H Coetzee, a commission was appointed on 13 June 1916 to inquire into and report on the advisability of altering the boundaries of the two game reserves and, generally, on matters affecting them. The commission was chaired by Mr J F Ludorf, and it was decided to visit the reserves to gain first-hand knowledge before proceeding to take evidence.

Wolhuter showed the commission the area round Pretoriuskop, and then de Laporte took them to parts of the western boundary (Klaserie River) and Sabie Bridge. Towards the end of the trip, a certain restlessness was noticed among the group, who were keen to do some hunting. A one-day shooting expedition was arranged and, after much walking and stalking, an animal was at last shot. Unfortunately it turned out to be a stray domestic cow from one of the neighbouring kraals, and a rather embarrassed official had to pay compensation to the owner. In spite of this farcical hunting expedition, every member of the commission was, apparently, a confirmed conservationist by the end of the visit.

Towards the end of 1918 the commission issued its report. It was extraordinarily favourable towards the reserves, and recommended that 'the policy of the administration should be directed towards creation of the area ultimately as a great national park where the natural and prehistoric conditions of the country could be preserved for all time'.

The report also recommended that there should be no reduction of boundaries and that the staff should be brought back to pre-war strength and augmented by two additional rangers. The only disappointment was the decision that the winter grazing of sheep was still to be allowed in certain parts of the south-west. At least, for the time being, the sanctity of the reserves had been secured.

Healy had been killed on active service in 1916 and de Laporte returned from the war in mid-1918. He was just in time to prevent Fraser, who was still acting warden, from being deprived of the warden's judicial authority. Some time earlier, Fraser had given up the warden's native commissionership. In fact, throughout the two and a half years of his acting wardenship, he had happily refused to do any sort of paperwork or record-keeping, and the internal affairs of the reserves had fallen into such disarray that an official of the administrator's department was about to be sent to take them over. It took de Laporte months to straighten out the mess.

The war years had not been good ones for conservation. With the staff reduced to half its strength, native poachers had operated freely and had sometimes spent weeks or months camped inside the reserves. The morale of the black police had deteriorated, and some of them had begun to overlook poaching. It was once again the task of Stevenson-Hamilton to restore order and direction. He had returned from the war with the rank of colonel and had immediately got down to work. He was faced with serious difficulties. The population of the Lowveld had continued to increase, land had become scarcer and more valuable, and the pressure on the reserves had mounted.

A coal syndicate, backed by strong government connections, had secured concessions for a few miles along the railway line to the north of Crocodile Bridge, and they started prospecting. The Railways themselves continued to demand that a settlement strip alongside the railway should be opened to farming. Farmers, having secured the right to graze their sheep in the buffer area near Pretoriuskop, wanted grazing rights much deeper in the reserve.

Most serious of all, the farmers to the south of the Crocodile River began demanding that suddenly 'unrivalled farming land' to the north of the river should be opened to settlement. They were backed by the principal land company. It started a smear campaign in the press, which made great capital out of the number of lions harboured in the reserve, which, it claimed, were a menace to farming.

All Stevenson-Hamilton could do was to hang on and fight for his beloved 'Cinderella'. One leading official in the administrator's department said to him, 'No doubt you will hang on year after year, and every year your reserve will be whittled away slice by slice, until one morning you will wake up and find the last bit has disappeared'. Stevenson-Hamilton discussed the matter with the chief clerk of the administrator's department. He suggested calling a conference of all the sections, government or other, who wished to cut up the reserves. At least the worst would then be known.

The meeting took place at the beginning of 1923 at the Old Government Buildings in Pretoria. One after another,

the delegates got up and stated their requirements, and the reserve got smaller and smaller. Eventually, Sommerville, the secretary for lands, rose to his feet and said, 'My department wants the whole Sabie Game Reserve abolished!' Things could not have been clearer than that, so, once again, Stevenson-Hamilton embarked on some discreet lobbying. An accomplished strategist, he first secured an interview with his principal adversary, Colonel Deneys Reitz, the minister of lands.

The meeting with Reitz was not unsatisfactory, as the minister agreed to visit the reserve in order to assess the situation for himself. The visit was scheduled for August 1923, and it was obviously crucial for the future status of conservation in the Lowveld.

Meanwhile, the Transvaal Consolidated Lands Company had bought up most of the privately-owned farms in the Sabie Game Reserve. Towards the end of 1922 they settled some 800 scrub cattle on their farm, Toulon, six kilometres from Sabie Bridge. Stevenson-Hamilton felt that the company's reason for doing this was to make life as unpleasant as possible for him, in the mistaken belief that he had the influence to persuade the government to buy out their farms.

The new manager of the farm was a Mr Crosby, with whom Stevenson-Hamilton quickly made friends and acquired a firm ally for conservation. In order to test their rights, the company instructed Crosby to do some shooting on the farm. Crosby told Stevenson-Hamilton of his instructions and was advised to proceed. With great deliberation he shot one wildebeest and then duly reported his action to Stevenson-Hamilton.

In the ensuing court action the defence pleaded that the wildebeest had been eating grass and that grass was a crop. (The game laws allowed property owners to kill animals caught destroying their crops.) The magistrate did not feel that grass was a 'crop' and gave judgement against the company. In the appeal to the High Court, the judge pointed out that he could not uphold such an argument, as it would mean the complete breakdown of all the game laws.

The court's decision had been the first positive development in favour of the reserve for some time. Another unexpected bonanza for conservation occurred when the Railways routed their 'Round in Nine' train tours to pass through the game reserve at night. Stevenson-Hamilton persuaded them to allow the tourists to spend one night at a siding opposite Sabie Bridge, and to remain there for the first hour of daylight. In return, his staff would provide a camp-fire for the passengers.

No-one was more surprised than the Railways when, at the conclusion of the tour, they learnt that the game reserve stop had been the most popular. It was later arranged that a game ranger would accompany each train, and take passengers for short walks at the various halts.

The camp-fires proved a great success. Tourists sang into the night and, every now and again, shivered in apprehension at the thought of the dangerous beasts that they imagined were watching them from just beyond the circle of firelight. One enterprising steward regularly dressed himself in a lion skin and, aided by some very realistic roaring from an SAP sergeant, rushed into the midst of each gathering. The more timid ladies shrieked with alarm, giving the bolder gentlemen the chance to assume protective stances.

Realizing the tourist potential of the game reserves, the Railways were quick to change their attitude to conservation. Even more important, it had been established beyond doubt that South Africans could derive considerable pleasure from viewing instead of shooting game. Armed with this evidence, and information on the popularity of the American national parks, Stevenson-Hamilton was in a much stronger position to fight for his 'Cinderella' during the scheduled visit of the minister of lands to the game reserve.

As arranged, Colonel Reitz, accompanied by Sommerville, arrived at Komatipoort in August 1923. Some members of the executive committee of the provincial council had also come, as had Dr Hjalmar Reitz (Colonel Reitz's brother), and Mr van Velden, the provincial secretary. Dr Haagner, the chairman of the Wildlife Protection Society (forerunner of today's Wildlife Society) was also present.

Stevenson-Hamilton met the party at Komatipoort and they travelled to Sabie Bridge by train. Throughout the trip several members commented excitedly on the game they saw beside the railway line, and discussed the sport they expected to have the next day. Apparently, before leaving Pretoria, the members of the executive committee had passed a special resolution giving themselves permission to shoot in the reserve. Stevenson-Hamilton lost no time in persuading the rest of the party to combat this move, and noted that a heated argument round the camp-fire continued late into the night.

The matter was dropped and the party enjoyed a pleasant week, during which they visited Saliji, Lower Sabie and Tshokwane. At Saliji, on a hint from Colonel Reitz, and as a gesture of goodwill, Stevenson-Hamilton took the members of the executive committee on a short hunt, and shot a wildebeest for food. When they walked up to the fallen beast, van Velden emerged from behind a bush, camera in hand, and announced that he had taken an excellent picture of members of the executive committee poaching in the reserve — a picture which might do well for the press!

By the end of the visit, Colonel Reitz was firmly in favour of the national park scheme, as was Sommerville, and

decided to approach the landowners without delay. Dr Schoch, legal adviser to the government, drew up a 'National Parks Ordinance', the Wildlife Protection Society began to campaign, and the Railways made 'Visits to the Reserve' a prominent feature of their Round in Nine tours.

As far back as 1913 it had been clear to Stevenson-Hamilton that the government was unlikely to approve expenditure on the purchase of all the two and a half million acres of privately-owned land in the Sabie Reserve in order to declare a national park. Accordingly, at the suggestion of Mr Rissik, he had drawn up a plan under which the area between the Sabie and Olifants Rivers was bisected by a line which roughly followed the meridian of 31° 30'. When Colonel Reitz approached Stevenson-Hamilton with the same suggestion, it was only a matter of defining on a map exactly which farm beacons should be followed.

And so, at the end of 1923, having sacrificed 64 000 square kilometres of the Sabie Game Reserve, (the best of the sable and roan country, all the Natal duiker, and nearly all the mountain reedbuck), Stevenson-Hamilton felt confident that the necessary legislation would be passed during the next session of parliament.

However, January 1924 brought a severe setback. He received a telegram from Reitz in Cape Town: 'National Parks Bill has been dropped'!

On the death of the prime minister, Louis Botha, in 1919, his close friend and confidant, General Smuts, took over the leadership of the South African Party. Botha had been in power since the first election after Union and had striven to reconcile the British and the Boers. Unavoidably, his efforts had alienated many of his own people and the South African Party began losing ground to the Nationalist Party under Hertzog. The Nationalist Party finally came to power in the general election in June 1924. Hertzog appointed P G W Grobler as minister of lands.

Towards the end of 1924 Stevenson-Hamilton called on Grobler for the first time. On the way to the minister's office, he tripped on a loose floorboard and sprained his ankle. Because of this omen, he had considerable forebodings about the coming meeting. But these proved unjustified. He found that Grobler, a grand-nephew of President Kruger, was already most sympathetic about the national parks scheme. He was also anxious to put the seal of permanence on his great relative's wish that land should be put aside where nature could remain unspoilt.

Sommerville had continued to be the secretary of lands and, once more, Stevenson-Hamilton felt optimistic about the future of 'Cinderella'.

During 1925 articles about the national parks scheme began appearing with increasing frequency in magazines and newspapers. Generally, the comment was favourable. However, towards the middle of the year, the campaign against the 'lion menace' was renewed with vigour. One Lowvelder wrote: 'I have lived here for thirty years, and we might have had a happy paradise of smiling homesteads, and what have we got instead? Lions!'

The campaign was not altogether unfounded, as lions did sometimes cross the Crocodile River in winter and kill stock. It appeared that the objective of the campaign was that 'certified sportsmen' should be allowed to enter the reserve and shoot lions. Realizing the problems this could cause, but at the same time not wishing to do anything to retard the national parks scheme at this crucial period, Stevenson-Hamilton secured the services of a Mr Harold Trollope to alleviate the 'lion menace'.

Trollope, a man with considerable hunting experience, was appointed ranger at Malelane. Within a few years he had shot all the lions in his section and most of those in neighbouring sections. He had a particularly cool nerve and, during the latter period of his lion culling, went out of his way to entice charges in order to make his work more interesting. Fortunately he never had rifle failure or a misfire!

As the year progressed, more and more people campaigned for the national parks scheme. The Wildlife Preservation Society did particularly valuable work in this respect, and a Mr Paul Selby was asked to send some of his wildlife photographs, taken in the reserve, to the houses of parliament. His pictures did much to stimulate the interest of members.

In August Sir William Hoy, the general manager of the Railways, deputed Mr Stratford Caldecott, an artist, to help promote the Sabie Game Reserve. Although he had no previous experience with wildlife, Caldecott soon became a champion of conservation. He spent two months at Sabie Bridge, and in this time quickly adapted to the veld and acquired a deep understanding of the issues at stake.

Caldecott spent a lot of time with Stevenson-Hamilton, planning how best to stimulate public interest in the reserve and also in the national parks scheme. During one of these conversations, Stevenson-Hamilton showed him the 1898 proclamation of the Sabie Reserve which had been signed by President Kruger. Stevenson-Hamilton wrote:

He looked hard at me, and catching on, I said at once, "Of course you are right, that is the obvious name – THE KRUGER NATIONAL PARK!" Few would be willing to oppose the founding of an institution linked with the name of the great President, and one felt that much of any opposition would thus automatically collapse. In truth also, it was the appropriate term, for as the records show, many years before the Sabie Reserve became a fact the

President had more than once spoken to apathetic gatherings of the necessity of game sanctuaries. Later, when the time seemed ripe, I asked some who were likely to have influence, to suggest it to the Minister, and I believe that is how the Park came to be known as it is today.

After returning to civilization, Caldecott immediately began publicizing the Sabie Game Reserve. Within a month of his return to Cape Town, hardly a person had not heard or read something about the reserve. His 'giraffe poster' appeared at every railway station in the Union and his articles in many newspapers and magazines. He addressed meetings and gave interviews to journalists. There was no one who worked harder to publicize the cause of conservation in South Africa.

As the year progressed, the major newspapers in Johannesburg, Pretoria and Cape Town devoted more and more space to the Sabie Game Reserve and its future. For the first time, the general public became aware of the issue and their reaction was increasingly favourable. The fight to establish the national parks scheme even found its way into the overseas media, and Stevenson-Hamilton began receiving letters of encouragement from all parts of the globe.

Meanwhile, Mr Grobler had devoted himself to organizing proclamation. In December 1925, he asked the representatives of the big land-owning companies to meet him for a final settlement.

The meeting took place in Johannesburg on December 9. Besides the minister, others present were Mr Schneider, representing the lands department, Major Scott (chairman of the Land Board), Mr HB Papenfus, KC MP, Stevenson-Hamilton, and the other land-company representatives.

The meeting was to be truly historic for conservation in South Africa. The minister opened with a conciliatory speech in which he pointed out that the national parks scheme was one outside politics. He suggested that it was everyone's duty to make sacrifices to ensure that the scheme would be successful. He stated that the government was willing to deal generously with the private landowners, exchanging their land inside the reserve for land outside its boundary, or paying cash, if this was preferred. However, he made it quite clear that those landowners who refused the offer would find their lands expropriated.

After all the years in the darkness, Stevenson-Hamilton left the meeting with a light heart. Here at last was a minister who was prepared to stand up and fight for 'Cinderella'. Of Grobler he wrote: 'No one else had done more than toy with the surrounding nettles, only when Grobler came along were they firmly grasped and the path made clear'.

If Stevenson-Hamilton's battle appeared almost over, the

minister's was just beginning. During the next few months he experienced a multitude of difficulties in procuring the necessary funds from parliament. If it had not been for his dedication, the bill would probably not have been laid on the Table during the first session, and any delay might have proved disastrous, as the opposition was beginning to organize itself. Various veterinary department officials began voicing their opinions that the tsetse fly still lurked somewhere in the depths of the Sabie Game Reserve, even though there had been no sign of it since the rinderpest epidemic of 1896. Colonel Reitz told the Kruger National Park Committee that he had recently met a deputation of two hundred sheep farmers who had expressed their indignation over the proposed national park. As a result of this and other events, he advised that the bill should be hurried on as fast as possible.

In April 1926 the select committee on Crown lands approved the exchanges necessary to constitute the Kruger National Park. On May 31 Mr Grobler moved the second reading of the National Parks Act in parliament. He made a long, eloquent speech in support of the bill, and explained his plan for putting the responsibility for the park on a board of control instead of the government:

> As long as the (Park) boundary is in the hands of the Government, the Government will always be exposed to being pressed by supporters to alter the boundary. Politics must be kept out of it. The danger is especially great that before a general election political influences will be brought to bear on the Government. Therefore, I propose the appointment of a board of control, representing the interests of the whole people. That board will have full control in its hands. It will be incorporated, and can sue and be sued. It will appoint its own officials, make its own regulations, control the Park, and in a word, act as the controlling body which has charge of everything in connection with the Park. The Board of Control will consist of ten members, serving for five years. Every year two will retire. I propose that eight members shall be appointed by me, one by the Transvaal Administration (because the Park is in the Transvaal) and one to be appointed by the Wildlife Protection Society . . . Eventually we shall get so far that each Province will appoint a member, the Government four, and the Wildlife Protection Society the tenth. Honourable Members will see that it is proposed that the members of the Board shall not be paid except for current expenses, such as travelling expenses. I want to say that the persons on the Board shall not make anything out of it.

General Smuts, the leader of the Opposition, seconded the motion. Amongst others who supported the bill were Mr H B Papenfus, KC, and Colonel Reitz. It was passed without dissent.

And so, after her precarious existence of the past twenty-one years, 'Cinderella' came of age. Telegrams and letters started pouring into Sabie Bridge, and Stevenson-Hamilton confessed to thinking he would have to buy a larger-sized hat.

Many had contributed to 'Cinderella's' upbringing, but it is hard to imagine that she would have had a future at all if it had not been for her champions: President Kruger, the father of the idea of game reserves in South Africa; Mr R K Loveday, who did valuable work during the 1898 and 1902 proclamations of the Sabie Game Reserve; Sir Godfrey Lagden, who helped Stevenson-Hamilton to accomplish so much in the two years after the Anglo-Boer War; H Stratford Caldecott, who promoted the Sabie Game Reserve and the national parks scheme; and the Minister P G W Grobler, whose dedication and action resulted in the passing by parliament of the National Parks Act of 31 May 1926.

After a struggle of more than twenty years, the swiftness of the proclamation came as a shock to Stevenson-Hamilton. He began to feel a little sad and depressed, as many parents do when their offspring reach maturity. It seemed that any further service would be in the nature of an anticlimax, and he decided that it might be best to say to the board, 'Here is the young lady who has been in my charge; I have done what I can to make her worthy of the position she is to hold; it is for you to see that she maintains it with dignity'.

Kind words and persuasion from Mr Grobler and a cable from the board as soon as it took over from the Transvaal administration eventually decided the issue for Stevenson-Hamilton. He was in Britain at the time and once more the ties of the Sabie proved too strong to break.

On his return, Stevenson-Hamilton found 'Cinderella' prospering under her new guardian, the board of trustees. He then set about making her more attractive to her prospective bridegroom, 'the Prince' — as he liked to call the public — and settled down to the everyday affairs of establishing this great national park. There were roads to be built, rest camps to be constructed, bridges and dams to be made, fences to be erected, and conservation measures to be introduced.

In 1928, when in London recovering from a bout of malaria, he met Hilda Cholmondeley. They were married two years later and had three children. Hilda had studied fine art in London and became well known for her paintings of African scenes, some of which hang in the Stevenson-Hamilton Memorial Library at Skukuza. (Sabie Bridge was renamed 'Skukuza' in 1936 in honour of Stevenson-Hamilton's services to the park.)

After guiding the destinies of the park for forty-four years,

Stevenson-Hamilton retired from the wardenship in April 1946 at the age of seventy-nine. He was succeeded by Colonel J A B Sandenburg in 1946; Mr L B Steyn in 1953; Mr A M Brynard in 1962; Dr U de V Pienaar in 1970; and Dr S C J Joubert in 1987.

Stevenson-Hamilton's successors have continued to build on the firm foundations he laid. Numerous developments have been necessary to accommodate the ever increasing demand from the public to visit the park. These developments have always been tastefully constructed and blended into their surroundings in keeping with Stevenson-Hamilton's wish that the park should remain an authentic wilderness. His sentiments were ably expressed by Hilda in a card she sent to friends on his retirement:

The Warden of the Kruger Park
Resigns in 1946.
Half a life-time spent with wild things
He has made it what it is.
With the help of splendid Rangers
And the approval of the Board,
Turned it from a wilderness
Into something world-renowned.
Essentially a Sanctuary
And the difference from a Zoo
Is that lions wander freely
Amongst the cars which contain you.
There is no such thing as vermin,
Nature rules unspoilt and free.
Woe betide the wicked poacher,
The Warden is his own J P.
So alone upon his kopje
As he bids farewell to his child,
He advises his Successor
"Keep it simple, keep it wild."

Wildlife Management in the Park

The Kruger National Park is world-renowned for its wildlife management. No other park in Africa has such comprehensive and sophisticated conservation facilities.

Although most visitors are aware of the Kruger's reputation in conservation, very few have any idea of how this vast area of African bush is managed. They may see a ranger driving by in a mud-splattered four-wheel-drive vehicle, a helicopter flying low over the veld, or a research or veterinary vehicle parked at Skukuza, and wonder what part each plays in nature conservation.

A man eminently qualified to answer all these questions is Mr Johan Kloppers, the head of wildlife management in the Kruger National Park. In this interview, Mr Kloppers was able to provide the author with a valuable insight into the practical side of wildlife management in the park, with particular emphasis on the role of the game ranger. A tall and extremely modest man, Mr Kloppers began his career more than thirty years ago when, at the age of twenty-two, he was appointed ranger of the Tshokwane section of the Kruger.

Aiken: *Can we begin with the early days of your career, as this will give some historical perspective to present-day wildlife management. Do you remember your first week as a ranger?*

Kloppers: That was in 1955. I started work in the Tshokwane section, which encompassed the whole area from the Sabie River right up to about ten kilometres south of Satara, including the Nwanetsi River on the eastern boundary. At the time there were only eleven rangers in the park, so each ranger was responsible for nearly 2 000 square kilometres. This was a huge area to have to look after as we had no helicopters or aeroplanes and there were very few roads. Everything I know about the bush, I learnt here; so my first week as a ranger was very tentative.

Aiken: *Did you soon become proficient at finding your way about?*

Left: Corporal Solomon Cubai and game ranger Mike English examine some spoor. Solomon comes from the village of Mapulangwene in Moçambique, and started working for Mike some eighteen years ago. The two men have built up a close bond of friendship and respect — an essential relationship for people who spend much of their lives walking through potentially dangerous bushveld together.

Kloppers: Yes, I had no choice. In those days, without even a decent map for reference, looking for pans and other topographical features on foot was extremely time-consuming. It's much easier for today's ranger to get to know his section. He can sit in his office and study a map or aerial photograph, then confirm his findings when he flies over the area. There are also lots of access roads: firebreak roads, patrol roads, and tourist roads. In about six months, today's ranger can learn as much as I could in five years.

Aiken: *Surely you must have had some basic maps?*

Kloppers: We had very few, and those we did have were so inaccurate that we couldn't depend on them. In fact, we had to draw our own. That's the reason why the walls of my office are covered in maps — I learnt to appreciate them!

Aiken: *Did you patrol on horseback?*

Kloppers: No, we didn't. When I started as a ranger, the era of horses was over. We had horses, but very seldom used them as they weren't bush-trained. We preferred to drive to a particular spot, then patrol the area on foot from there. We did often use donkeys for carrying our equipment into offroad areas.

Aiken: *Were your donkeys ever attacked by lions?*

Kloppers: Lions are generally afraid of people during the day, and unlikely to attack donkeys when there're people around. But it was a different matter at night, and we had to tie our donkeys to trees, and build a few fires and a little kraal of thorn branches around them.

Aiken: *During your early days as a ranger, was patrolling your only duty?*

Kloppers: It was a full-time job. You didn't know how many animals of the different species you had on your section, you could only estimate from the spoor. A good example is what was then known as the western boundary trek game. This consisted of thousands of wildebeest and zebra, and it was impossible to estimate their numbers with any accuracy. We didn't know where they came from, or where they went to. I eventually found out by stationing my game scouts in the trek game's winter grazing-ground. The game scouts had to wait for more than a month, until one night in September it rained. The next morning all the animals were gone. They had started trekking to their summer grazing-ground. My game scouts followed the spoor, and within twenty-four hours were north of the Orpen Gate. That was the first time we realized that the trek game moved up and down the western boundary for more than sixty kilometres from south to north. Unfortunately, I never had the opportunity to witness this migration from the air. It was not until 1963/1964 that we started using helicopters and, by that time, the western boundary trek game had considerably decreased as a result of the boundary fence which had finally been erected in 1961.

Aiken: *Can you recall the first significant change in your duties as a game ranger?*

Kloppers: Changes were gradual. One very important task was the making of patrol and firebreak roads, which opened up more and more of our sections to vehicles.

Aiken: *Was it a ranger's task to decide where these roads were to go?*

Kloppers: Yes. It was quite an easy decision to make, as there were no roads. We were guided to problem areas, and areas we wanted to enter for specific reasons. We made hundreds of kilometres of patrol roads that eventually evolved into firebreak roads. All our roads were made by hand as we had no bulldozers.

Aiken: *Before the boundary fences were erected, how did you prevent farmers on the boundaries from poaching?*

Kloppers: There were very few farmers, and they had so much game on their own farms that there was little temptation to poach in the park. We did have some poaching in certain areas where we still have poaching.

Aiken: *When was the radio introduced and what difference did this make to your life as a ranger?*

Kloppers: Colonel Stevenson-Hamilton had already introduced radios before I started. These were old air-force M17s, which could not be used in our trucks. Our radio sessions were much more formal than they are today because the rangers were so far apart. On the other hand, there was less obligation to attend radio sessions as we were often in the bush, away from our radios. In those days, rest camps were closed during the rainy season. It's only recently that we have had tourists throughout the year, making it necessary for a ranger to be readily contactable.

Aiken: *Over the years, tourism and the number of employees working in the park have considerably increased. Has this resulted in a ranger having to spend more time on administration duties and less on patrolling his section?*

Kloppers: No, but the work intensity has certainly increased. In my early days as a ranger, if I wanted to travel from A to B to do some task, it could take two or three days or a week. Today it takes half as long to get there, or even less. Sometimes you needn't even go at all because you flew over the area on the previous day. With modern methods we can often accomplish much more in the same period of time.

Aiken: *Would you say all changes in the park have been beneficial?*

Kloppers: No, I wouldn't. In those days we had no fences; now we are fenced in. Should we have problems with epidemics or droughts, we are now completely reliant on our own resources. Animals can no longer move freely out of the park in times of need. For instance, during the rinderpest epidemic of 1896, a lot of species in the Lowveld were just about wiped out, but pockets of them survived in Moçambique and began to filter back. We didn't attach so much importance to some of the things then, that we worry about now. Nature could be left to look after itself. I actually believe we were much better off then, even though we knew less.

Aiken: *Would you say that there is more game in the Kruger today, than when you first started work as a ranger over thirty years ago?*

Kloppers: Yes, there is. We have less wildebeest, and probably less zebra, but there are many more elephant, and many more of virtually any species you can name. When I started working at Tshokwane, there was only one herd of elephant in my section. This was the only breeding herd south of the Olifants River. The herd never moved south of the Timbavati River until 1958/59, when it drank in the Sabie River for the first time. Then, in 1961, we held a hippo count. In those days hippo counts were done on foot. The rangers started at the Sabie Gorge on the Moçambique border, and walked westwards along the river. They had to run away from elephants so many times that they eventually started counting them instead of hippo. They counted what was then considered a vast total of 104 elephants along the Sabie River.

Aiken: *It must have been virtually impossible to estimate the elephant population in the thick bush between the Sabie and the Crocodile Rivers using only ground counts. When did you do your first aerial census?*

Kloppers: If I remember correctly, we did our first aerial census in 1964 using a fixed-wing aeroplane. We counted something like 350 elephants in the south, and 3 000 in the entire park. It was at that stage that we first anticipated that culling would become necessary. Since then, the elephant population has increased rapidly, although we keep it within a thousand either side of seven thousand, for management purposes. It's interesting to note that the increase was not entirely natural, as the human population explosion in Moçambique forced many elephants to move into the Kruger.

Aiken: *Before we discuss the daily routines of modern wildlife management, could you briefly describe how nature conservation decisions in the Kruger are made. Perhaps you could also indicate the place of research in these decisions?*

Kloppers: Nature conservation in the Kruger Park consists of the research division and the wildlife management division. Decisions are made collectively. In-depth research is usually done first, then management and research, together with the park warden, form the policy. This policy is referred to a management committee, and then to the National Parks Board of Trustees, who have the final say.

Aiken: *Who is responsible for implementation once nature conservation policies have been made?*

Kloppers: Wildlife management is mainly responsible for implementation, and the game ranger is our key implementary person. At present, there are twenty-two game rangers managing the park's vast area of 19 485 square kilometres. Each ranger has his own staff, and is responsible for wildlife management in his area. This includes the implementation of policies, and enforcement of the Parks Act and regulations laid down by the board.

Aiken: *You mentioned that in-depth research usually precedes management decisions. Dr Pienaar, the chief executive of the National Parks Board, has defined the objectives of research in the Kruger Park as 'defining and explaining the natural processes governing the ecosystem, so that staff can accurately plan the park's management'. What sort of research is being done in the Kruger Park?*

Kloppers: Most of our research is management-orientated. For instance, if we foresee a problem, we ask our scientists to research it. Research is necessary to decide on or facilitate such things as veld-burning policy, whether we should supply water to a certain area, culling, game capture, etc.

It's impossible to decide what to conserve without knowing what one has, so a vital and ongoing task of research has been to compile an inventory of everything in the park: vegetation, soils, drainage systems, mammals, birds, reptiles, insects, etc. Compiling inventories was more important in the early days of research, the fifties and sixties but, as data accumulated, the emphasis moved more to monitoring. Our aim has been to build up a reference of what needs to be protected, why it needs to be protected, and only then to formulate policies.

Aiken: *What about research that is not management-orientated?*

Kloppers: This is usually undertaken by visiting scientists. Very often there are more 'external' than 'internal' research projects on the go in the park.

Aiken: *How does research that is not management orientated benefit the Kruger?*

Kloppers: For every external research project undertaken, we have our own input, as we oversee these projects. Some of the information so gained can be applied immediately, some only in the future, some never. All knowledge, however, is welcome — we have a commitment to research.

Aiken: *It is clear then that contemporary wildlife management in the Kruger is heavily research-orientated. The romantic image of the game ranger overseeing his domain on horseback, and experiencing countless adventures, has been replaced by a highly qualified wildlife manager. What qualifications must a ranger applicant possess?*

Kloppers: A matric (standard ten), is the minimum requirement. We prefer a ranger to seriously aspire to getting the three-year Diploma in Wildlife Management or a BSc. The diploma will eventually be the required minimum qualification. Even if an applicant has this qualification, he will not necessarily get the job. We try to assess the individual, and not just look at his qualifications. If we believe we have the right man, the qualifications can always be acquired later.

Aiken: *What sort of qualities do you look for?*

Kloppers: Self-reliance is very important. We look for some-one with a well-balanced personality. Self-esteem is also essential, because he may have to live alone for long periods. If he's married, his wife must be able to cope. He must realize that in eighteen out of twenty-two sections his children will go to boarding-school. It's very important to know the dis-advantages.

Aiken: *What about experience in the bush?*

Kloppers: As there are very few places where the practical experience we need can be acquired, we do not consider previous experience really necessary. We actually prefer our chaps to gain their practical experience in the Kruger. With our present policy, we don't immediately appoint rangers to a section. They are first appointed as wilderness trail rangers. The advantage of this is that it gives us time to evalu-ate and select the most suitable section ranger candidates. Looking after eight trailists helps one to become more responsible. Trailists also motivate one to extend one's theoretical and practical knowledge.

Aiken: *Is this because trailists continually ask questions?*

Kloppers: Quite so. If a trail ranger has had two years on trail, he's literally been on foot in the bush for a full year. The knowledge acquired in those two years, because of its intensity, will exceed any knowledge that I gained in three times that period.

Aiken: *Once a ranger has been selected, and entrusted with managing a section of the Kruger, what do you see as his most important duty?*

Kloppers: The ranger's primary duty is, and always has been, to get to know his section. This is imperative if he is to manage it effectively.

Aiken: *With your rangers spread over such a large area, how do you keep in touch with what they are doing, and forward instructions to them?*

Kloppers: Every morning, from Monday to Saturday, we have a radio session at seven o'clock where each ranger in turn reports in. In this way, not only is there communication between Skukuza and the individual rangers, but each ranger can listen in to what is going on in the rest of the park. This is not formal reporting, but more along the lines of the rangers discussing what they have done over the past twenty-four hours, and what they intend doing that day. One of

the nice things about being a ranger in the Kruger is that, unless you have been asked to do a specific task, you decide on your own daily work schedule.

Aiken: *For some years now, all the rangers have had radios fitted to their vehicles. What are the reasons for having a radio session every morning, rather than each of the rangers reporting in when it's convenient to him?*

Kloppers: You know, if you have twenty-two chaps dis-persed through the bush over 20 000 square kilometres, you need something that binds them together. The chances of me, or even the chief ranger, seeing a particular ranger more than once a month, are small. We don't see some of them for two or three months at a time. So one must have voice contact, just to let them know you are there, and so they can ask for advice. For me, it's important to know that every-thing is all right.

Aiken: *The Kruger ranger is often envied by colleagues in other parks because of the considerable resources available to him. These include helicopters and fixed-wing planes; a research division, including the veterinary section; work-shops situated strategically throughout the park; and a road-building contingent. In addition there are also various small sections under the wildlife management division that help the ranger manage his area — if only indirectly. Could you elaborate on the role of these sections?*

Kloppers: There is the traffic section, which sees to the implementation of the rules and regulations affecting tourists. There is a section looking after the maintenance of fences on the boundaries. There is pollution control, which is concerned with the pollution of the veld by exotic plants, and also with the disposal of rubbish coming out of the rest camps. There is also a small section consisting of two instrument-makers who are primarily concerned with the production and maintenance of instruments, darts, and darting-rifles which are used in game capture and culling. They also maintain our ordinary rifles.

Aiken: *Does the traffic section do the speed-trapping in the park, or is this done by provincial traffic officers?*

Kloppers: The Kruger has its own laws and regulations, so provincial traffic officers have no jurisdiction in the park. Our own traffic officers spend a lot of time on speed con-trol. This is not very popular work with the public but, unfor-tunately, it's the only way to stop people speeding and endangering the animals. Our traffic officers have quite wide

Above: There are few people as important to conservation in the Kruger Park as Hugo van Niekerk, the chief pilot of the National Parks Board. Hugo flies both fixed-wing planes and helicopters for tasks such as game capture, culling, aerial census, aerial photography, anthrax inoculation by darting, and taking officials on inspection tours of remote areas.

powers in enforcing the park's act and regulations, especially those relating to tourists. This includes looking for people who drive off roads, litter, feed animals, and contravene other similar regulations.

Aiken: *To what extent is law enforcement the concern of the ranger?*

Kloppers: He enforces the national parks act and regulations as well as our own code of conduct, and is the disciplinary head of all personnel in his section. He must be aware of everything that goes on in his area, for instance, personnel driving off the normal roads, driving after hours, etc.

Aiken: *Is he in charge of the rest camps in his section?*

Kloppers: No, he is not in charge, but is responsible for discipline in them. A ranger cannot interfere with the management of a rest camp but, should the tourist officer have trouble with a drunk or rowdy tourist, or should there be an accident or theft or something of this nature, the ranger will be called on in his capacity as law-enforcement officer. This is one of the reasons why he must be so readily available.

Aiken: *Does law enforcement vary much from section to section? For instance, some of the rangers have sections without tourists but with quite a bit of poaching.*

Kloppers: Very true. It balances itself out. There are few sections that have neither one nor the other. The further you go away from the normal tourist areas, the nearer to the park's boundaries, the more poaching there normally is.

Aiken: *Does a ranger devote much time to tourist control outside the boundaries of the rest camps?*

Kloppers: During patrols, he makes sure that tourists don't drive off the roads, get out of their cars, and generally break any of the park's regulations. The rangers share this responsibility with the traffic section.

Aiken: *So the ranger has to be a bit of a diplomat as well?*

Kloppers: Oh yes. Although he is backed by the law and must be strict, there is no advantage in hammering a person too hard. In any confrontation situation, one has to tread softly in order to reap the benefits that one is looking for.

Aiken: *We have dealt with the responsibility of a ranger to know his section and enforce the law. Could you now list the main components of the effective wildlife management of a section, and then could we discuss each one separately?*

Kloppers: The effective wildlife management of a section encompasses many duties. The more important would be: fire control, water provision, animal diseases and problem animals, culling, and combating poaching.

Aiken: *Before the advent of man, natural fires, such as those caused by lightning, must have often burnt vast areas of veld before being halted by natural impediments. Man has changed the face of the land and has imposed many obstacles to natural fires. He also frequently starts veld fires, either accidentally or deliberately. What is the main objective of the Kruger's fire-management policy?*

Kloppers: Our aim is to simulate a natural fire regime as far as possible. We have a policy of controlled burning, which is implemented by the rangers. The rangers also have to combat accidental fires. We have a lot of fires caused by lightning, poachers, illegal immigrants, and even by tourists.

Aiken: *We have discussed the building of dirt roads to function primarily as firebreaks. For practical purposes, aren't all roads, especially the wider tourist roads, effective firebreaks?*

Kloppers: Yes, that is so. The result of our comprehensive road network, including tourist, firebreak, and patrol roads, is that the park is divided into more than 400 separate blocks of veld of varying size for fire control and management purposes.

Aiken: *On an average, this means that there are about eighteen blocks per ranger's section. How does the ranger use these blocks to control fires?*

Kloppers: Most firebreaks are roughly six to nine metres wide, which is far too narrow to prevent veld fires from crossing should there be a wind behind them. The firebreaks

do, however, give a clear line from which to burn back and so stop the main fire. They enable rangers to control accidental fires, as well as fires on blocks that have to be burnt according to the prescribed schedule.

Aiken: *There are experimental burning plots alongside roads in several parts of the park. How are these plots of use to management?*

Kloppers: The first experimental burning plots were laid out in 1954, and included plots in the four dominant vegetation types. The plots consist of blocks of veld each about 200 by 400 metres, surrounded by firebreaks. The blocks are laid out alongside each other beside a firebreak or tourist road. One of the blocks is usually kept as a control block with no burning at all, and various fire regimes are simulated in the other blocks. Some are burnt in winter, some before rain, some after rain, some are burnt with as hot a fire as possible. Botanists make regular checks on the plots, and feed all the data gained into our computers. We are then able to calculate the effects of the various fire regimes.

Aiken: *How much say does a ranger have as to which blocks in his area should be burnt each year?*

Kloppers: Quite a lot. According to our policy, the frequency with which blocks are burnt is determined by rainfall. Once it has been determined what proportion of each landscape type is to be burnt, the relevant blocks are called up with the assistance of a computer. However, before these blocks are actually burnt, one of the botanists and one of the management people go and inspect the blocks in the presence of the local ranger. It's only possible to see so much in a day, so they have to rely heavily on the ranger's intimate knowledge of the area. If for some reason he believes a block shouldn't be burnt, he sets out his case and normally the others agree.

Aiken: *Do you have a lot of problems with fires started outside the park?*

Kloppers: Many of our neighbours believe in burning the veld every year. If we didn't have firebreaks along our boundaries, these fires would often cross into the park.

Aiken: *Does today's ranger still have a say in where new firebreak roads will go?*

Kloppers: Oh yes, with his local knowledge, he will help select the route for a firebreak, and then go and peg it out.

Aiken: *Do you still make a lot of firebreak roads?*

Kloppers: We already have over 4 000 kilometres of these roads, and have just about reached the limit. One of our problems in the park is soil erosion caused by our firebreak roads. We can't gravel them all at this stage, so they are mainly graded roads which pass through all sorts of terrain. Last year, and the year before, we had a lot of washaways, and the rangers had to spend considerable time repairing these. Consequently, we are a bit reluctant to extend our firebreak network. We first need to consolidate what we have.

Aiken: *The Kruger is blessed with six major perennial rivers: the Limpopo, Luvuvhu, Letaba, Olifants, Sabie and Crocodile rivers. Unfortunately, all of these rivers originate to the west of the park, and so are susceptible to contamination and water usage from the outside. How much of a problem is this?*

Kloppers: It's a serious problem. All our perennial rivers pass through agricultural and/or industrial areas before entering the park, and the majority of these areas are becoming increasingly populated. As a counter-measure, we have built weirs and dams in some of our rivers, well realising this to be a short term solution only.

Aiken: *Could you give a few examples of contamination and reduced flow?*

Kloppers: One of the most serious instances was in January 1983, when the sluice-gates of a dam outside the park were opened. Hundreds of tons of sludge were washed downriver causing the Olifants River to clog up in places. Many thousands of fish and other river creatures died as a result. When something like that happens, it takes years before river life is back to normal. More worrying is that, in recent years, perennial rivers such as the Luvuvhu, Crocodile, and especially the Letaba, have on occasion stopped flowing.

Aiken: *As you have said, human populations in many areas to the west of the park are rapidly increasing, as is their water consumption from the Lowveld's major perennial rivers. In the light of this and the Kruger's history of serious droughts such as that of 1970, which resulted in the deaths of many animals, what steps has the National Parks Board taken to ensure the adequate provision of water for the wildlife?*

Kloppers: Apart from our river systems and dams, we have over 400 windmills supplying about 350 strategically-located water-points. It sounds a lot to say there are 350 water-points, but extended over 20 000 square kilometres, they just disappear.

Aiken: *With water-points scattered throughout the park, wildlife management must have a powerful tool for manipulating game movements. For instance, do you often close off the water supply in an overgrazed area so that game will move elsewhere?*

Kloppers: We only do this in exceptional cases. One of the most important benefits of having these windmills is that during drought periods we don't have to worry so much about rare species, such as roan antelope and the recently re-introduced Lichtenstein's hartebeest, being harmed by the more robust species.

Aiken: *Who maintains the windmills?*

Kloppers: All the rangers have windmills on their sections; the ranger at Vlakteplaas, for instance, has about forty on his. Although the rangers are not responsible for major repairs, they have to look after normal daily maintenance such as the greasing and oiling, the pulling-up of pipes, examining cylinders, and other similar jobs. This is not one of their more popular duties.

Aiken: *Couldn't a ranger's time be better spent on more important matters?*

Kloppers: Ensuring that there is sufficient water for the animals is very important, so rangers regularly check all water-points themselves. This includes inspecting and determining water levels in dams, reservoirs and troughs, as well as making sure that all windmills are in working order. If we were to appoint technicians to do this, we would need eight to ten of them in a full-time capacity just to be as efficient as we are now. Having the rangers looking after the windmills is just a practical solution. Should there be a major repair required, the ranger will radio for a technician.

Aiken: *You mentioned the rinderpest epidemic of 1896, which had devastating results on the animal population of the park. Should a similar epidemic occur, animals are now contained within the park's boundary fences. The early detection and eradication of disease is, therefore, very important. What routine methods of disease detection do you use?*

Kloppers: Our rangers take blood smears from all carcasses found in the veld. They also keep a constant look-out for sick and injured animals, and have the authority to catch or shoot these animals for examination. A lot of useful information is also acquired during culling operations.

Aiken: *Who analyses the blood smears?*

Kloppers: This is done by the veterinary section, which consists of our own veterinary officer, his full-time assistant, and a vet seconded from the army on an annual basis. There is also a state veterinary section with its own functions and responsibilities.

Aiken: *What is the function of the state vets?*

Kloppers: Their main work is to detect and research animal diseases which affect domestic animals. For instance, foot-and-mouth disease is of little danger to wild animals, but can have grave consequences if transferred to domestic cattle. The state vets check all culled carcasses in the veld and make sure that those with symptoms of foot-and-mouth or other diseases are not taken for processing. The state vets are also in charge of hygiene at the processing factory at Skukuza.

Aiken: *What about diseases which are a danger to wildlife?*

Kloppers: These are mainly the concern of our own veterinary section. Let's consider anthrax, for example. Domestic animals can be inoculated against this disease, but it would be impossible to inoculate all the wildlife in the park. In 1960 we had a serious outbreak of anthrax which spread rapidly through the northern half of the Kruger, killing many animals. The disease is carried by flies, vultures and other scavengers which have fed off contaminated carcasses. In order to contain the outbreak, we had an enormous task burning carcasses, burning large tracts of contaminated veld, and treating infected water supplies.

Aiken: *How badly did the disease affect your stocks of rare species?*

Kloppers: Our roan antelope population was seriously depleted. Nowadays, however, we immunize most of the roan population each year by firing darts containing vaccine into their rumps from helicopters. The darts also contain a marker dye, which leaves a coloured patch on their coats as confirmation of immunization.

Aiken: *What sort of problem animals do you have?*

Kloppers: There are always animals that make a habit of breaking the boundary fences and raiding crops outside. Elephant cow herds seldom break through our so-called 'elephant fences' on the eastern boundary, but large bulls can. Some of them get out of hand and wander continually to and fro. We normally cull these bulls first during culling operations.

Aiken: *What other problem animals do you have?*

Kloppers: We quite often have to cope with wounded animals, mainly in areas along our boundaries, such as along the Crocodile River. The animals cross over into neighbouring farms, where they are hunted. When they are shot at, or break out of snares, they normally quickly return to the park. If wounded, some of the larger animals such as lion, buffalo, and elephant can become dangerous, not only to the rangers and their staff on foot patrols, but even to tourists. Rangers are often forced to shoot these animals. Larger animals which have been wounded in fights can also be very dangerous.

Aiken: *Could you give an example?*

Kloppers: When one talks specifically of dangerous animals that have been injured in fights, one is bound to think of the hippo. Hippo bulls often fight, inflicting large wounds on each other. These wounds are irritated by nibbling fish and water, so the bulls stay on land while their wounds heal. A hippo out of water feels very insecure, and becomes highly unpredictable and dangerous.

Aiken: *I believe that you once had to shoot an injured hippo in self-defence. What happened on that occasion?*

Kloppers: We found the hippo out of water, lying down. A hippo on land doesn't know the meaning of a mock charge. If he charges, he sees it through. This particular hippo was no exception. He hears you, then sees you, then comes straight for you. You shout to try and scare him off, but it doesn't work, so eventually you have to shoot him.

Aiken: *Culling has become an important part of wildlife management in the Kruger. Who is responsible for the culling?*

Kloppers: We have introduced a policy whereby every ranger must do the culling on his section. The reason for this is to share out the unpleasant tasks. Culling is an important job, and it must be done efficiently and humanely.

Aiken: *What animals do you cull?*

Kloppers: We cull mainly buffalo and elephant, and do this by shooting the animal with a scoline dart from a helicopter. Scoline is a tranquilliser, and in the case of buffalo, the overdose kills them before the ground crew can reach them. Elephants are shot with a rifle as soon as they are down.

Aiken: *How many animals do you cull at a time?*

Kloppers: With buffalo, we normally do between thirty and forty at a time. With elephant cow herds, eight to sixteen at a time, and in the case of elephant bulls, only two to four per day.

Aiken: *Is the quantity of animals culled limited to the number that can be transported back to the processing depot that day?*

Kloppers: Yes. The only reason we cull in the Kruger is for management purposes. Once this decision has been made, we believe that products from culling should be utilized as efficiently as possible, and the proceeds from sales of these products ploughed back into nature conservation. The decision to cull is never primarily for the product. Even if we have a surplus of certain species, we will not interfere unless nature cannot cope. For example, during the seventies we had a high rainfall period, and species such as impala, kudu and giraffe increased considerably until there were far too many of them; but we weren't worried about it. As soon as there was a food shortage due to drought, their numbers dropped to realistic levels, without having harmed the habitat or associated species. However, where there are large animals such as buffalo and elephant that don't have serious predators, they cannot be left to multiply until nature takes its course. By the time elephants started dying because of drought, they would have harmed the habitat to such an extent that large numbers of associated species, such as roan antelope, would have been completely wiped out.

Aiken: *Most herds number far in excess of the forty buffalo or sixteen elephant culled at a time. This means that very often only part of a herd is culled. How do you separate this section of the herd?*

Kloppers: It's relatively easy to cut off part of a herd. We fly low over them and, as they scatter into groups, select the group to be culled and herd it with the helicopter towards the culling site. This location is chosen because it's easily accessible to the vehicles which must carry the culled

carcasses back to the processing depot. Usually it's next to a firebreak, well away from tourist roads. Once the culling site has been reached, the helicopter circles the animals, and keeps them in a group and in one place. The ranger, who sits behind the pilot, then fires scoline darts from a modified 20-gauge shotgun into two of the animals. While he reloads, the helicopter continues to circle, keeping the animals in a tightknit group. This procedure continues until all of them have been darted and have collapsed. The ranger then radios the ground crew, who have been waiting at a safe distance. They then move in and shoot any animals that are still alive.

Aiken: *How many people are there in the ground crew?*

Kloppers: There's the culling supervisor, and a field staff of about twenty who do the butchering and loading once the state veterinary representative has inspected each carcass. The ground crew are directly responsible to the processing depot.

Aiken: *Are there scientists present?*

Kloppers: Yes, our scientists often join up with the ground squads, but they're not a permanent part of the team. We try and get as much information as possible out of culling.

Aiken: *Could you give a few examples of the sort of information scientists are able to obtain?*

Kloppers: Animals can be aged by examining their teeth. This allows scientists to calculate the different age structures. An examination of the foetuses enables the calculation of gestation periods as well as gestation rates. All this sort of information is very useful to us. Sometimes visiting scientists are present. We even had Chris Barnard collecting an elephant heart to see how it worked.

Aiken: *What effect do you feel culling has on the survivors of the herd?*

Kloppers: There is a disturbance factor but, fortunately, this disturbance factor, or the fact that the survivors are afraid of the helicopter, is not associated with man or vehicles. Even though the remainder of the herd tend to move

Overleaf: The Kruger Park's 27 000 buffalo are distributed throughout the park. Controlled culling of the large herbivores has become necessary to prevent them from multiplying to the extent that they harm the habitat.

out of the immediate area temporarily, they remain in their normal walking territory. We do worry about the disturbance factor, but there's nothing practical we can do about it. As yet we have no alternative. We believe our method of culling is as efficient as it can be. I think it says a lot for our organization that, in an area as large as the Kruger Park, we go out and select the animals to be culled, cull them, and then transport the carcasses up to 300 kilometres to the processing depot, all in the same day.

Aiken: *Do you ever capture buffalo or elephant calves as a by-product of culling operations?*

Kloppers: Buffalo are carriers of foot-and-mouth, and can't be sent out of the park. We do sometimes bring in elephant calves alive. These are sold or given to other conservation bodies, like the Natal Parks Board, or the Pilansberg Nature Reserve.

Aiken: *Would these calves have to undergo quarantine?*

Kloppers: Yes, or they always have had to in the past. Elephants have recently, however, been taken off the foot-and-mouth list and quarantine for distribution in South Africa is no longer required.

Aiken: *Over the past few years, poaching in Africa has changed dramatically. The population explosion, civil wars and a general lack of agricultural development have led to widespread poverty and food shortages, even famine. This has placed an increasing burden on wildlife stocks, not only from the traditional type of poacher who snares or shoots food to feed his family, but more especially from a new breed of poacher whose only motive is profit. Perhaps what has facilitated this new type of poaching is the easy availability of automatic weapons, particularly AK47s. In Zambia and northern Zimbabwe, bands of poachers armed with automatic weapons have frequently fired on conservation officials. Has this happened in the Kruger?*

Kloppers: Yes, we've had quite a few skirmishes with ivory poachers in recent years.

Aiken: *Anti-poaching patrol under these conditions must be very dangerous. When you learn of one of these infiltrations, how large a counter force do you send out?*

Kloppers: It depends on the incident. At one stage, elephant poaching along the Moçambique border increased to such an extent that we had to combine all our resources to combat it. The poachers normally worked in twos and threes, or even larger groups, so to have only one ranger up against them would have been a bit short-sighted. Large groups were used, and in 1984 we established a specially trained para-military body of rangers to combat these incursions. We have now reduced elephant poaching to manageable proportions.

Aiken: *Approximately how many elephants have been poached in the last few years?*

Kloppers: We lost about 180 bulls over the 1982 to 1984 period. However, during 1985, we lost only one on the Moçambique border and four on the western boundary. The western boundary was a new area for elephant poaching, but we managed to curb it very quickly. It's relatively easy to curb poaching when one has access to the areas where poachers live. But, where poachers can cross an international boundary, they can't be pursued. We got to the stage where we knew who they were, where they lived, and all about their operations, but our hands were tied. That's the reason elephant poaching reached the proportions it did.

Aiken: *Automatic weapons are usually of a relatively small calibre. Has poaching with these weapons resulted in many wounded elephant in the park?*

Kloppers: We normally only find elephants days or weeks after they have died, and by then it's often very difficult to detect bullet wounds. All in all, I wouldn't say we've had a lot of wounded elephants, except when poachers have fired into herds. Fortunately this has only happened on a few occasions.

Aiken: *In the 1983/84 annual report of the National Parks Board of Trustees it was stated that only five elephants were poached in the Shingwedzi area during the second half of the year. This was attributed to the dismissal of certain Moçambiquan game scouts. What happened in this instance?*

Kloppers: Our game scouts weren't actually doing the shooting, but supplying poachers in Moçambique with information. The problem was that the game scouts had families in Moçambique, and, as a result, were open to intimidation. After these game scouts were dismissed or transferred, there was an immediate reduction in elephant poaching.

Aiken: *The present situation has meant more police and military personnel along our borders than in the past. Has this drastically reduced poaching?*

Kloppers: The police and army are always on the lookout for poachers, but that's not one of their main duties. Our rangers and game scouts, on the other hand, meticulously patrol the boundary areas for poachers. There is very close liaison between the rangers, the police and the army and this is beneficial to poaching control.

Aiken: *In recent months there has been a flow of refugees from Moçambique crossing the park illegally in order to reach the homelands in South Africa. Has this had any impact on meat poaching?*

Kloppers: In the past the total number of animals poached for meat in the park in a year was minimal. One pride of lions would probably have killed more animals in the same period. A very different type of meat poaching now occurs. This is largely due to the presence of illegal immigrants on the Transvaal side of the park, and the famine and civil war in Moçambique. It's no longer a case of someone who hasn't had meat for a month coming into the park in search of something to eat. Instead, poaching is now a business. These poachers kill as many animals as possible, and then sell the meat outside the park. This poaching is as bad as ivory poaching.

Aiken: *If you look back to when you first started working in the park, would you say that developments in wildlife management have been beneficial to the ranger?*

Kloppers: Oh, yes. He attains a high standard of knowledge more rapidly than in the old days. But I wouldn't change what I had — it was much slower, there was no hurry. One thing the chaps don't have today is tranquillity.

Aiken: *There must have been a considerable sense of adventure, as roads were few and far between?*

Kloppers: Yes. But even so, that is relative. Nothing in the bush has changed. The fact that you have more roads is immaterial. You can get to a spot faster but, once you leave the road, you are in the bush, and the bush is the same. One is inclined to imagine the bush was wilder in former times. In reality it hasn't changed, but has only become a bit more accessible.

Aiken: *How do you envisage the ranger of the future? Will developments in research and technology greatly change his duties?*

Kloppers: No, I don't think so. I can see that eventually the sections will become smaller but, as long as the park remains the same size as it is now, I can't see the work of a ranger changing very much. There might be more pressure on the boundaries in future, more pressure as far as poaching is concerned; but the ranger's primary duties of getting to know his section, law enforcement and implementing management's policies will remain the same.

Aiken: *To conclude, could you summarize the ideology underlying wildlife management in the Kruger?*

Kloppers: Our basic policy is never to interfere unless we have to. Unfortunately, because of the park's long narrow shape and the fact that it is entirely fenced in, it is not a completely balanced ecological area. As a result, we sometimes have to step in and assist nature. In certain circumstances, even if we decide to do nothing about a problem, that is a management decision. On the other hand, one can do a lot of damage by shying away from problems, particularly where one is working with dominant things like elephant, buffalo, fire, water or the lack of it. When we make a management decision, and the implementation of that decision results in usable products, such as carcasses from culling, our policy is to utilize those products and plough the proceeds back into conservation. The decision to utilize the products is always secondary, our primary decision is the management one. If we have to interfere, our aim is to simulate nature as closely as possible.

Wilderness Trails

Few of us have the chance to experience the thrill of an encounter on foot with big game, or to enjoy the mental tranquility that a stay in the wilderness can bring. The Kruger National Park's wilderness trails offer just such opportunities.

Since the establishment of the Wolhuter trail in 1978, the demand for wilderness trails in the Kruger Park has been so great that three more have been established, and others are on the drawing-boards.

In order to learn more about the Kruger Park's wilderness trails, the author was fortunate in obtaining this interview with David Chapman, one of South Africa's most experienced trail rangers.

Aiken: *Many would say you lead an ideal life. How did you become involved in wilderness trails?*

Chapman: I've been walking in the bush for about thirty years. In 1956 I started working for the Game Department and the Colonial Police in what was then the Bechuanaland Protectorate. During this period, I was the first game ranger in the Chobe district, and also worked in such interesting places as Maun and Ghansi. In 1968 I returned to South Africa and met Ian Player. He was a great influence on my life, and I started going on trails and then taking out trails for various organizations in areas in Zululand and Natal. I joined the Wilderness Leadership School as senior field officer in 1977, and in 1983 started as a trail ranger in the Kruger Park. My objective was to help establish the Bushman's trail.

Aiken: *A trail ranger has a highly responsible job as his actions and decisions can jeopardize the lives of the people on trail with him. Most trail rangers will not have had your wealth of practical experience when they start working in the Kruger. How does the National Parks Board ensure that they are sufficiently qualified in this crucial practical sphere?*

Chapman: Professional trail rangers take trainee rangers on trails and this gives novices valuable field experience and a first-hand knowledge of the different aspects of trailing.

Left: A crocodile suns itself in the Olifants River below the Olifants wilderness trail camp. A short distance upriver, the attractive 'pothole' rock formations act as a barrier to fish trying to swim upriver to spawn. Large numbers of crocodiles often congregate in this stretch of river to feed on the trapped fish.

It's important to make sure that a ranger is fully competent to protect a trail. In order to accomplish this, he is given extensive firearms training, and is also subjected to simulated charges by some or all of the potentially dangerous animals. His reactions to these charges are of great importance.

Aiken: *What is the maximum number of trailists allowed on trail?*

Chapman: Our trails are normally booked well in advance, so most of them have the maximum of eight trailists, in addition to the trail ranger and his assistant.

Aiken: *Do both rangers carry firearms?*

Chapman: Yes. Normally all trail rangers are armed with a .458 magnum. I obtained permission to carry a .375 because of my preference for that calibre. My colleague carries a .458.

Aiken: *Do people usually book for trails as part of a group, or is it also possible for individuals or couples to reserve a place on a trail?*

Chapman: Most trails are booked by groups, but there are also many individuals who come on trails and who don't know any other trail members at the outset.

Aiken: *Are all trails of the same duration?*

Chapman: Yes. Trails consist of three nights at the base camp, and two days of walking. For example, if a trail started on the first of the month, you'd leave on the afternoon of the first, and be back on the morning of the fourth.

Aiken: *What equipment should one bring?*

Chapman: We supply all the food, bedding, towels, as well as beverages such as tea, rooibos, coffee, 'Fresh-up' fruit juice, and water. Trailists must bring their own alcohol, cooldrink preferences and minerals. Basically we supply everything except clothes and toiletries.

Aiken: *What sort of food do you provide?*

Chapman: Good simple food. Let's take the three main meals. We might have buffalo stew on the first night, then

chicken curry with rice and vegetables and salads on the second, and a braai with lots of meat, stywe pap, sheba, and salad on the final night. It's usually almost midday when we arrive back from our morning excursion, so for lunch or brunch or whatever you like to call it, we have a substantial meal of eggs, bacon, sausages, toast, etc. The only meal that isn't substantial is breakfast, as we carry it with us. For breakfast we have nutritional food that we can take on the walk, like peanuts and raisins, 'Fresh-up' fruit juice or maybe some dry boerewors.

Above: Trailists sleep in attractive thatched huts built on stilts to ensure better ventilation during the hot summer months.

Below: Rifle over his shoulder, trail ranger Dave Chapman leads a trail through some interesting countryside next to the Olifants River.

Aiken: *Do you cater for people with special dietary needs?*

Chapman: If people inform us in good time, then we cater for them. But if they arrive on the day of the trail and tell us that they're vegetarian or that they only eat kosher food, there's often not much we can do about it.

Aiken: *Should trailists wear camouflage clothes?*

Chapman: Wildlife is colourblind, and only sees in terms

of shades of black and white. If one wears a particularly flashy shirt, it will stand out as a darker black or a lighter white. In my opinion, the colour of clothes is not that important.

Aiken: *What sort of footwear do you recommend?*

Chapman: Most people wear trackshoes or comfortable soft boots. I use both, and spend a lot of money on quality footwear. If possible, people should stick to footwear that they're used to. New shoes can be fatal!

Aiken: *Is physical fitness important when one goes on trail?*

Chapman: Trails are not an endurance test, but a wilderness experience. On the other hand, we have had people who, after a few hundred metres, haven't been able to walk any further. We walk at an easy pace, and usually cover ten to fifteen kilometres in the morning, and perhaps two to six in the afternoon.

Aiken: *Isn't that a bit far for elderly people?*

Chapman: I walk to suit the most unfit person in the group. There's an age restriction of twelve to sixty, but on special application we do get older people. I once had a lady of seventy-eight and she walked the trail without any problem, but she was very fit.

Aiken: *In most instances would a party of older people book out the entire trail?*

Chapman: Yes, this would often be the case. If it isn't, one needs to strike a happy medium, and the young people must be satisfied with walking slower and not so far. In any case, I myself walk slowly.

Aiken: *What sort of people come on trails, and for what reasons?*

Chapman: A broad cross-section of society comes on trails – mainly South Africans. People come for diverse reasons and to satisfy different needs. Some come on trail to get away from it all; others are avid wildlife-lovers and/or amateur conservationists. Quite a few stumble across trails by chance, and find they like them. In all the years I have been trailing, I have never met anyone who didn't enjoy a wilderness trail, except when a person has become ill or injured and had to stay in camp.

Aiken: *Do you often get trailists with specialized objectives?*

Chapman: The majority of people, when filling in their trail forms under the heading 'What is your special interest?', write 'everything' or 'general'. If there's any group who specifically wants something, it's the bird-lovers. There're lots of them, because ornithology is one of the few aspects of nature that can be studied in an urban environment.

Aiken: *It's sad to think how few areas there are left in Africa where one can have a true wilderness experience. How do you feel a Kruger trail compares to others that you have known?*

Chapman: Apart from the few other game reserves where there are trails, the Kruger Park can't be beaten in South Africa and probably in southern Africa for a trail that is led by a professional ranger. Trailists stand a chance of seeing all the so-called 'big five', plus an extraordinary diversity of flora and lesser fauna.

Aiken: *What is the extent of your responsibilities to trailists?*

Chapman: Well, firstly, we have to protect the trail. I don't want to give the impression that every time we walk out of camp, we are subjected to attacks from wild animals, but it can happen. My responsibility is to try and see that situations don't arise which will endanger the trailists and the animals. I also believe that a wilderness trail can be a learning experience, but I don't force this on trailists. A lot of people just want to relax and enjoy walking through the bush and seeing big game at close quarters. However, if a person has a more puristic trail in mind, we will be only too happy to oblige. After all, there's no better vehicle from which to peddle conservation, than wilderness trails.

Aiken: *What aspect of trail ranging gives you the most pleasure?*

Chapman: I get a lot of satisfaction from seeing the joy and excitement when I'm able to show people what they want to see. Many people come into wild country, with its natural rhythms and cycles, with complete misconceptions. When I offer them a good wilderness experience, I see these attitudes changing, and have the thrill of opening up new perceptions and avenues of thought.

Aiken: *You mentioned that you feel wilderness trails are one of the best vehicles from which to peddle conservation. Could you expand on this?*

Chapman: You know, there's much talk about environmental education in the classroom. I don't really believe you can teach it that way. I believe one has to experience nature in the raw. A lot of people will say we are preaching to the converted, but that's not the case. We get all kinds of people on trail. For example, I remember when eight employees of a certain company had been sent on a trail and didn't really want to be there. They were frightened, and brought a lot of liquor to bolster their confidence. Much to their surprise, they loved the experience so much that the company sent another eight people.

Aiken: *Can you describe a typical trail, such as the Olifants, from beginning to end?*

Chapman: I meet the trailists at three o'clock on a Monday or Friday afternoon, at the pick-up point in the Letaba rest camp. Let's say it's Monday and winter. We go into the trails office, and I collect their indemnity forms and any money still owing to the National Parks Board. I then show them on the map where we will be entering the wilderness area, where the base camp is, and also give them a brief description of the countryside. We then embus after loading all our gear onto the Land Rover's trailer.

Once we have entered the wilderness area, I usually stop and we stretch our legs before travelling the final few kilometres to the base camp. On arrival at the camp, I show them the facilities and huts that they are to use. Once they have unpacked and organized themselves, we get together round the camp-fire for a drink and talk.

At this stage, I let them know what the schedule is going to be for the duration of the trail, and also explain the rules and regulations of the camp. I tell them that the camp is theirs for the duration of the trail, and that they must relax and enjoy themselves and make use of the facilities as much as possible. I ask them not to hesitate to come to me if they have any problems or complaints, and also remind them that they may not leave the camp without me. We then discuss walking in the veld. I explain that, in their best interests, I'm very strict in the veld, and that they must be prepared for this. When I give an instruction, it's non-negotiable and non-debatable. I then talk about a wilderness trail, what it is and what it isn't, and about the qualities of wilderness. I try to suggest to them how they can get the most out of their trail. I inquire if anyone has a special interest, and also let them know that I'm always prepared to attempt to answer any questions. By the time we've had supper, most people are ready for bed.

Next morning I make sure that everyone is awake by five o'clock. We have tea or coffee and rusks, and I try to get

on the move by six o'clock. Depending on the area we want to walk in, we either walk there directly, or drive there. The wilderness area is so vast that, if I want to utilize certain parts of it, there's no alternative but to drive and then walk. We usually spend about five or six hours out trailing, then return to camp. Trailists then have a drink and a shower, and brunch is served. After this, most people sit about and watch wildlife or birds, or sleep until we go out again in the afternoon.

In winter we leave on the afternoon walk at about three o'clock. I try and make a point of walking out of camp at least twice, and usually do this in the afternoons. We don't walk very far, and may end up sitting on some vantage point watching hippos and crocs and water-fowl or, where there's no river, something else. I don't plan far ahead because I don't like a trail to be regimented in any way. In fact, I encourage people to leave their watches in their huts and to forget about time. I leave our return to camp as late as it's safe and usually come in just before dark.

Generally people are more talkative on the second evening and all sorts of things, from the stock exchange to exotic holidays, are discussed around the camp-fire. Very often, trailists ask questions until late, while others prefer to relax and listen to the sounds of the night.

The next day is basically a repetition of the previous one, but I try to show trailists different areas of the wilderness so that they can experience a diversity of landscape. On the final afternoon we walk very little. I try to find a high vantage point and to get trailists to sit in silence and absorb the wilderness and reflect on the trail. We watch the sun go down and then return to camp at dusk.

On the last night the conversation tends to be much more relaxed, as rapport has normally been established between ranger and trailists. Next morning we have breakfast at about seven o'clock and then drive back to Letaba rest camp.

The following trail goes out on the Friday afternoon and comes back on Monday morning.

Aiken: *Could you tell us more about the instructions you give trailists prior to taking them into the veld?*

Chapman: I ask them to keep in as compact a group as possible, and to walk in single file. This is something that I check up on all the time, because my colleague and I walk in front.

Aiken: *Isn't it rather unusual for both rangers to walk in front, instead of one in front and one behind the trail?*

Chapman: I believe it's very important to have both guns in the front for a number of reasons. Firstly, experience has

taught me that the trail is more likely to be attacked from the front, or from the side near the front. If my colleague is at the back, it's almost impossible for him to do any shooting because he has the trailists in front of him. Also, when both rangers walk in front, it prevents mini-trails developing. For instance, someone at the back will find a spoor and will ask the ranger what it is, and stop to examine it. Then, before one is aware of it, four or five trailists are half a kilometre behind. Even more important, if the second ranger walks at the back, his motivation becomes virtually non-existent. He eventually walks watching the heels of the person just ahead of him, and takes no active part in the proceedings.

Above: Sunset, and the day's adventures are discussed round the campfire. Trail ranger Dave Chapman, on the right, explains a point to a captivated audience.

Right: While trailists relax round the fire, a skilled cook prepares a tasty meal.

Overleaf: Walking through the magnificent and very rugged geomorphology of the Olifants Gorge, is an experience few trailists forget. The gorge's quiet isolation imparts the atmosphere of the true wilderness.

Aiken: *Have you always had both rangers in front on your trails?*

Chapman: I once put my number two behind the trail for a month, just to prove the point to him. As soon as I returned him to the front, there was a noticeable change in his attitude. He enjoyed the trail more and obtained more job satisfaction. Sometimes he points out rare plants that I've seen, but didn't bother to show the trailists because they weren't receptive. In fact, he quite often stops the trail because I have overlooked something that he feels the trailists should see.

Aiken: *How important is the relationship between the two rangers?*

Chapman: It's very important that you should like and respect each other. When I'm in the veld with my number two, we can communicate extensively with just a glance, and this is vital in crisis situations. In order to achieve this type of working relationship, I believe you have to have an easy and friendly relationship when not on trail. This can't be forced on two people. If it doesn't exist, it's probably better for both of you to try working with someone else.

Aiken: *After you have told trailists that they must walk in single file and keep in a compact group, what else do you tell them?*

Chapman: They must not talk while they are walking. Naturally I stop from time to time to point out things, and allow the trailists to stop me whenever they want to ask something. Even then, I try to keep voices subdued. This is not only to hide our presence from animals that we might come across. I find the sound of the human voice in a natural environment intensely repugnant.

Finally, I give them instructions on what to do in the unlikely event that we're charged. I keep the instructions extremely simple, and prepare them psychologically and physically. I tell them that they must forget about preconceptions such as climbing trees, crawling down ant-bear holes, or disappearing into the distance, and advise them to keep behind me and my number two. In other words, they should keep the rangers between the attacking animal and themselves. They must also stay in a close huddle. I repeat these instructions several times, and then illustrate what would happen if we were walking and an animal attacked from the side. My colleague and I would turn and step out to meet that animal, and the trailists would have to come round and get behind us. The second important instruction I give them is that, if things get really critical and happen very fast, such as a full charge from close quarters, I will tell them what to do and they must do it immediately and without thinking. I explain to them that in Johannesburg I need someone to look after me; in the bush, they need me to look after them.

Aiken: *You mentioned earlier that, on the first night, you tell people about the qualities of wilderness and how they can get the most out of the trail. Could you expand on this?*

Chapman: I tell them that a wilderness trail is not a big-game spectacular, that it's far more than this. I appreciate their desire to see exciting animals that are potentially dangerous, and will do my best to find these animals. But that's only a part of a wilderness trail, and they must look upon game as a bonus. Some people think that, if you walk through wild country, you'll see more game than if you drive. I explain to them that this is not true. With a wilderness trail, the accent is on the quality of the experience.

When you're in a car, you have a visual experience. If you hear anything, it's the engine, or the sound of people talking or shouting with excitement. And that's all you have. But, on a wilderness trail, you see, you hear, you smell, and sometimes touch. I tell the trailists that I will try to guide them into at least one quality experience. It's very different viewing a herd of zebra from a car to stalking them carefully, watching them watch you, hearing them snort and then gallop away, their hooves pounding on the ground and kicking up dust. It's one thing looking at a lion from the safety of a vehicle, but another walking round a bush and suddenly finding yourself face to face with one. There's nothing between you and the predator but the rangers. The lion's eyes are hot and yellow, and seem to be burning right through your skull, and you feel the adrenalin surge through your veins. Then the beast gets up and grunts and runs away, and you get an incredible impression of grace, beauty, and power, and you feel an exhilaration that's hard to explain. You'd never get that from a car.

I also point out the economic value of wilderness, and how that might save it. It's got aesthetic value — just open your eyes, your ears, and your nose and you'll be aware of the beauty of wild country. It has therapeutic value. There's probably no better environment where man can recharge his soul. And, I suggest to them that, encompassing all these things, the wilderness has a spiritual value, and leave it at that. I don't expand on the spiritual aspect because I don't want to offend anyone. I tell them that the wilderness will speak far more eloquently than I can.

Aiken: *How safe do you feel trailists are?*

Chapman: I tell my trailists that there is no chance that an animal will succeed in passing both me and my number two and reaching them. Should an animal attack me, my number two will shoot the animal. Should it attack my number two, I will shoot it. We've had several unfortunate incidents on trails. I have personally had to shoot two animals on consecutive trails. One was a lone buffalo which, for trail purposes, is probably the most dangerous animal. The other was a hippo.

Aiken: *Are those the only two animals you have had to shoot during all your years of trailing?*

Chapman: In thirty years of walking in the bush, I've been charged a number of times, but have only had to shoot on those two occasions.

Aiken: *What happened in the incident with the buffalo?*

Chapman: The buffalo was sleeping concealed in some long grass to the right of the trail, and I actually walked past without seeing him. I knew there was a buffalo ahead, but was concentrating on a stream on the left where there were mud wallows. If my number two hadn't seen the buffalo, the back part of the trail would have been charged and somebody could have been killed.

Aiken: *What did you do when your colleague pointed out the buffalo?*

Chapman: The buffalo was only a few paces from me; all I saw was a bit of hide. I slowly backed the trail away. The next thing I saw was the buffalo coming from about ten paces. That's a very short distance to be charged by a buffalo, and we put the animal down about five paces from the two of us.

Aiken: *Where did you shoot him?*

Chapman: My first shot went in just underneath his chin and knocked him down. Then, as is normal with dangerous animals, we made certain with a few well-placed shots.

Aiken: *Why do you think he charged you?*

Chapman: We were too close to him, and he probably felt threatened. I find the Kruger buffalo, especially the lone bulls, more aggressive than any others I have come across.

Aiken: *What happened in the case of the hippo?*

Chapman: A lot of people consider the hippo to be the most dangerous animal in Africa. I'm not going to give an opinion. In this case, the hippo had probably been involved in a territorial dispute because it had large bite marks on its hide. It was about a metre from water, facing the water, when we passed it at a relatively safe distance.

Aiken: *How far from it were you?*

Chapman: About forty metres. It then walked into the bush and we lost sight of it. I left the trailists where they were and walked forward with my number two to have a look at the hippo. We found it standing behind a bush watching us. I decided to leave it alone and we walked back to the trail. The hippo then came out of the bush and, even though there was water only a few paces away, decided to charge us. I shouted at it, picked up a piece of wood and threw it at it, and it still kept coming. I was left with no alternative but to shoot the animal. My first shot killed him and I put two further shots in his head just to make sure. He was only five or six paces from me when he dropped.

Aiken: *A trail ranger spends much of his working life walking through the bush. Day after day, he comes into close contact with potentially dangerous animals, and must learn more about how they react under various circumstances than practically anyone else. As one of southern Africa's most experienced trail rangers, which animals do you consider the most dangerous, and what do you take into consideration when approaching them on foot?*

Chapman: There is a big difference between hunting an animal and approaching it on trail. If you are hunting, and you wound either a lion or a leopard, then I believe you have the two most dangerous animals on your hands. But we're talking about trailing. On trail I would say that the buffalo is the most dangerous animal, followed by the hippo in areas where you regularly find them out of the water, such as the Olifants trail area in winter. I don't worry about hippos too much in summer, because they're just about always in the water, and will seldom leave it to attack you. I've only had that happen once.

Aiken: *How do you find the social classification of animals affects their behaviour towards man?*

Chapman: With all dangerous animals, their behaviour varies considerably according to their social classification.

For instance, breeding herds of elephant are very dangerous, whereas bachelor bulls are easier to approach. Contrarily, breeding herds of buffalo are far less dangerous than solitary bulls. Where lionesses are with their cubs, this is a highly volatile situation. If you get too close to a leopard, you stand a good chance of being attacked.

Aiken: *You have classified the solitary buffalo as the most dangerous animal one can encounter on trail. What thoughts do you have, and what actions do you take if you meet one at close quarters?*

Chapman: It's always vitally important to be aware of the wind direction when you're trailing, because animals react very strongly to man's scent. So the first thing I would do is stop the trail and check the wind direction to see if it has changed from my last check. Then I would study the buffalo's reactions. If it makes any attempt to close the gap, I back the trail away and leave the animal alone. If there's no attempt to do this, I may allow trailists to take pictures. I feel there's a critical distance, closer than which you should not approach dangerous game, unless certain things are present, like a stream. I don't believe this distance is twenty or a hundred metres, you have to judge each situation separately. Once you approach closer than this distance, the animal will either run off or charge. The more a dangerous animal feels threatened, the more likely it is to retaliate. Ideally, one should be able to approach an animal, let the trailists view it, and then withdraw without the animal becoming aware of your presence. This seldom happens.

Aiken: *People often learn a lot about themselves in dangerous situations. Does this apply to a close encounter with a dangerous animal?*

Chapman: When an elephant turns around and looks down his trunk at you, that's a quality experience. If people are a bit apprehensive, so much the better. It does them a lot of good because they will get over the fear later. I don't think there's anything like wild country to bring a man down to size. Arrogance quickly disappears.

Aiken: *Could you describe the different attractions of each of the Kruger's wilderness trails?*

Chapman: Let's take the Nyalaland trail first. Trailists meet at the Punda Maria camp, which lies to the south of the wilderness trails area. En route to the trail camp are the massive and spectacularly coloured Shantanalani sandstone formations. The trail camp is situated in a shady spot next to the Madzaringwe stream, a short walk from the Luvuvhu River. Without doubt the trail is a bird-watcher's paradise. Not only are there several species endemic to the area, but most of the birds found in the park are found there. Of special interest are the black eagles which nest in the cliffs overhanging the Luvuvhu River. The area also has one of the greatest varieties of plant species found anywhere on earth.

Aiken: *What would you consider the scenic highlights, and what animals are to be found there?*

Chapman: The riverine vegetation along the Luvuvhu River is spectacular country to walk through. There are also some impressive views from cliffs overlooking the river. The wilderness area is rich in baobab trees, and in one place there is a plateau of them − almost a large forest − which has a very special atmosphere. Apart from the usual species of wildlife, this is a good area to see eland, roan, sable and nyala.

Aiken: *Moving southwards, could you describe the Olifants trail next?*

Chapman: As we discussed, trailists meet at the Letaba camp, and are driven to the wilderness area which lies to the south-east of the Olifants camp. The trail camp overlooks the Olifants River, and is only a few kilometres to the west of its scenic confluence with the Letaba River. The area offers a wide diversity of terrain. It's on the edge of the Lebombo Mountains. It also has gently undulating basalt plains dissected by streams which drain into the Olifants River. These streams hold good deep water for hippo and crocodiles, and are lined with attractive riverine trees. Away from the streams, you have a rugged type of bushveld with small bushes and trees which are generally thorny and have hard leaves so as not to lose water in this low-rainfall area. Then there's the magnificent and very rugged geomorphology of the Olifants and Bangu Gorges.

Aiken: *This seems to be one of your favourite areas.*

Chapman: It's a very popular trail, and in my opinion the trail where you're likely to see the most game. It's not unusual to see all the 'big five'. An interesting feature of the area is the river immediately below and to the west of the trail camp. Over the ages, the Olifants River has carved a multitude of unusual shapes out of the rocks that line its bank and over which it often flows, including the spectacular 'pothole formations'. These 'potholes' act as a natural barrier to fish trying to swim upstream to spawn. Consequently, hundreds of crocodiles often congregate in this small stretch of river to feed on the trapped fish. We don't give guarantees but, if we did, this is one area where you can be sure of seeing crocodiles.

Aiken: *The Wolhuter and Bushman trails are the two southern-most trails. Could we discuss the Wolhuter first?*

Chapman: Trailists meet at Skukuza, and are driven to the wilderness area, which is to the north-west of the Berg-en-dal camp. The trail camp is well shaded, and has a waterhole nearby. The area has no major perennial rivers, but has several annual streams, such as the Mavukani. The terrain consists of undulating plains and surrounding rugged hills and dome-shaped granite outcrops. The plains are much more undulating than those on the Olifants trail, and are dominated by combretum and marula trees. It's an all-round trail with good game-viewing and birdlife. One can be very lucky there, and on some trails I have seen more game there than even on the Olifants trail. This is one of the best rhino areas in the park.

The Bushman trail has a very special place in my heart, as I helped establish it. The wilderness area is south of the Wolhuter trail, and trailists meet at the Berg-en-dal camp. The trail camp is only seven kilometres from the Wolhuter camp, and also has its own water-hole. The vegetation and topography are much the same as the Wolhuter trail, but it's generally more mountainous. Dotted about are attractive granite koppies with their greys and whites and pinks and other colours, which subtly change as the sun rises and sets. As its name implies, the area is rich in anthropological and archaeological interest. Stone Age tools, implements and clay pots are easy to find, and there's a lot of Bushman rock art. These rock paintings are of great interest as they show the type of animals that existed in the area a thousand or more years ago. Of course, some trailists want to see more of this than others. Some don't want to see it at all, and they don't have to. The game and bird life is more or less the same as that on the Wolhuter trail, but in some of the more mountainous areas klipspringer and mountain reedbuck are more easily seen. There are also a lot of rhino in this area.

Aiken: *Would you like to conclude with a few thoughts on conservation and wilderness trails?*

Chapman: Many people who are not involved in conservation believe that conservationists are oddballs. Nothing could be further from the truth. In the long run, the most important aspect of conservation is conserving the human race. The most important natural law on earth is interdependency. If one asks a person from the city about the functions of a tree, he'll probably start talking about beautiful furniture. But trees manufacture oxygen, they recycle water into the atmosphere, and also provide food. You can't live without oxygen for more than a few minutes, without water for more than a few days, and without food for more than a few weeks. Look what's happening around the globe. A lot of our oxygen is manufactured by plant plankton in the sea, but oil slicks and pesticides are affecting the plankton. We're cutting down forests at an amazing rate — look at the Amazon, look at Africa. The real energy crisis here in Africa is not the threat of another Arab oil embargo or higher oil prices, but that trees are being cut down for firewood and are not being replaced. Fortunately, I think people are becoming more aware of conservation. If we destroy plant life on earth, we destroy ourselves — it's as simple as that!

In my opinion, the greatest value of wilderness trails is their therapeutic value. Man was once a hunter/gatherer, and lived in a natural environment with its harmony and natural rhythms and cycles. I believe we have a deep-seated or subconscious desire to return to the peace and harmony of that environment. If you take people out on trail and just walk in the veld and look at animals, that's all they're going to get out of the trail. But, if you talk to them about the qualities of the wilderness, and about the great religious leaders who retired to the wilderness for periods to think and to recharge their souls, this makes the trail more meaningful. Man is a spiritual animal, although we may not know this any more, so the wilderness says something to us. I'm probably biased, because I'm a committed Christian; but I think it's very relevant that Jesus went off into the wilderness on many occasions so that he could commune with the Creator, with his Father. I don't like holding court in camp; I like to show people living examples of creation — the more subtle nuances — otherwise they don't see them. It's not my place to force this on trailists, and I don't. But, when they are responsive, they stimulate me, and I run a better trail. Sometimes people literally leave on a high. I've had trailists burst into tears at the end of a trail because they didn't want to leave.

The Southern District

Skukuza

Pretoriuskop

Jock of the Bushveld

Berg-en-dal

Malelane

Crocodile Bridge

Lower Sabie

Tshokwane

Left: Skukuza has a resident population of over 3 000 park employees. In the foreground are some of the more than 200 tourist huts, and in the distance the large staff village with its nine-hole golf-course.

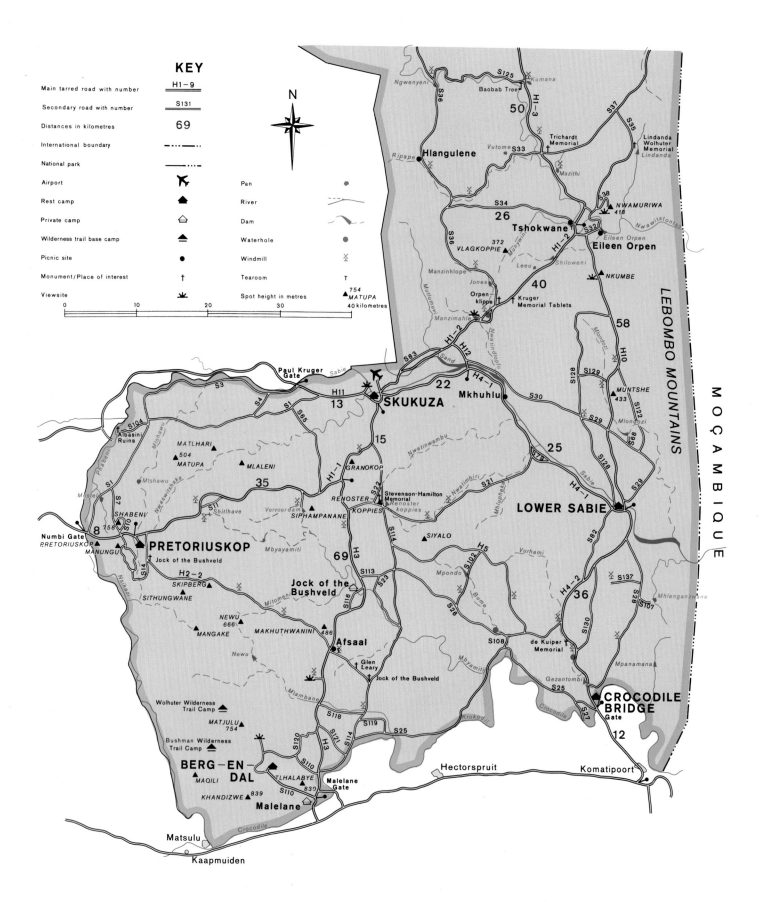

KEY

Main tarred road with number	H1–9		
Secondary road with number	S131		
Distances in kilometres	69		
International boundary	–––––		
National park	––·––		
Airport	✈	Pan	●
Rest camp	▲	River	
Private camp	△	Dam	
Wilderness trail base camp	▲	Waterhole	●
Picnic site	●	Windmill	⚒
Monument/Place of interest	†	Tearoom	T
Viewsite	✹	Spot height in metres	▲ 754 *MATUPA*

0   10   20   30   40 kilometres

N

MOÇAMBIQUE

LEBOMBO MOUNTAINS

Ngwenyeni
S125   Kumana
S36
Baobab Tree
50   H1–3
Ripape   Hlangulene   Vutome   S33   Trichardt Memorial   S37   S35   Lindanda Wolhuter Memorial
Mazithi   Lindanda
S34   S38
26   NWAMURIWA 418
Tshokwane   S32   Eileen Orpen
S36   372   H1–2   Eileen Orpen
VLAGKOPPIE   Leeu   Shiloweni
Manzinhlope   40   ✹ NKUMBE
Jones
Orpen-klippe   58
Kruger Memorial Tablets
Manzimahle   H1–2   H12   S128   S129   MUNTSHE 433
H10   S122
S83   Sand
Paul Kruger Gate   Sabie   H4–1   S30   S29   Mlondozi
H11   22   Mkhuhlu   Nwatinwambu
13   ✈ SKUKUZA   S79   25
15   Nwatimhiri   S128   Sabie
H1–1   Granokop   S22   S21   H4–1
35   RENOSTER   Stevenson-Hamilton Memorial   LOWER SABIE
Mtshawu   Shitlhave   KOPPIES   Renoster koppies
Albasini Ruins   MATLHARI   MLALENI   SIPHAMPANANE   S114   Mhlanbeni   S82
S104   504 MATUPA   Vervoerdam   SIYALO   Vurhami
Mshetl   S1   Mtshawaka   Mbyayamiti   69   H3   H5   Mpondo   Bume   S137
Phabeni   S7   SHABENI   S113   S102   H4–2   36
Numbi Gate   758   S23   Mitomeni   S26   S108   de Kuiper Memorial   S28 S107
PRETORIUSKOP   8   S10   PRETORIUSKOP   Jock of the Bushveld   Mbyamiti   Mhlanganzwane
MANUNGU   S14   H2–2   Jock of the Bushveld   AFSAAL   S30
SKIPBERG   S116   Glen Leary   Gezantombi
SITHUNGWANE   MAKHUTHWANINI 486   Jock of the Bushveld   S25
NEWU 666   AFSAAL   Mpanamana
MANGAKE   Newu   CROCODILE BRIDGE Gate
Mlambane   S118   S119   S25   Crocodile   S27
Wolhuter Wilderness Trail Camp   12
MATJULU 754   S120   S121 S114
Bushman Wilderness Trail Camp   S110   H3
BERG–EN–DAL   S110   Hectorspruit   Komatipoort
MAQILI   TLHALABYE 830   Malelane Gate
KHANDIZWE ▲ 839   Malelane
Matsulu   Crocodile
Kaapmuiden

54

Skukuza

A short drive from the Paul Kruger gate and on the southern bank of the Sabie River, Skukuza is the largest camp in the park. Steeped in history, the camp is also the park headquarters.

In spite of its size, Skukuza has managed to retain the tranquillity and atmosphere of old Africa. The camp's superb layout leaves most visitors entirely unaware of the adjacent staff village, which houses more than 3 000 park employees, and the numerous administrative buildings and workshops, which have been tastefully blended with the surrounding bush.

Skukuza's thatched huts and cottages can accommodate over 500 visitors, and the camp site more than 600. The camp boasts two restaurants, a post office, a library, a bank, an airport, public telephones, an open-air cinema, and the headquarters of the Automobile Association in the park. The camp also has a small supermarket, a petrol station and an information office.

The most sought-after accommodation lines the Sabie River. Well-shaded lawns stretch from these huts down to the river bank, ensuring superb views of the river and of any animals coming down to drink.

A popular gathering-place for visitors is the large open veranda outside the main restaurant and cafeteria complex. The veranda overlooks the river, and from it visitors can often see animals such as hippo, crocodiles, bushbuck and an occasional buffalo bull. The sycamore fig trees in front of the veranda offer exceptional bird-watching when the figs are ripe. Green pigeons and purplecrested louries are particularly prominent and allow a much closer approach than normal as they feed off the juicy figs. From September to March large breeding colonies of masked weavers nest in these trees.

The countryside round Skukuza consists of relatively thick bush dominated by thorny acacia thickets and red bushwillow trees. The camp offers the visitor a wide choice of game drives and for this reason is a firm favourite.

The most popular drive from Skukuza is eastwards on the H4-1. The road follows the southern bank of the Sabie River and is lined by luxuriant riverine vegetation on the one side and thick bush with occasional small open spaces on the other. A number of loop roads down to the river offer a chance to see hippo and crocodiles.

A wide variety of animals can be seen during the drive. Impala, giraffe, warthog, kudu and buffalo are common. Always popular with the visitors are the troops of baboons which sun themselves beside the road in the early mornings. The non-stop antics of the younger baboons can keep one amused for hours.

Less common but also seen regularly near this road are bushbuck, elephant, lion and hyaena. Elephant are most likely to the east of the Mkhuhlu picnic spot. Visitors should also keep a lookout for leopards sunning themselves in the trees alongside the river.

Another excellent route is to cross the Sabie River on the H1-2 and head towards Tshokwane. A clan of spotted hyaenas lives near the bridge and in the early mornings they can often be seen returning from a night's hunting. Lions are also usual beside this road.

As one proceeds northwards the mixed combretum veld opens out and makes game-viewing much easier. Herds of impala and waterbuck are common and buffalo, giraffe, kudu and warthog are seen regularly. Wildebeest and zebra become more plentiful as one nears Tshokwane. Keep an eye open for klipspringer when passing the rocky outcrops in the vicinity of the Kruger tablets.

Many visitors breakfast at the Tshokwane picnic site and tea-room before returning to Skukuza on the same route. I recommend taking the S34/S36 loop and spending some time at the Manzimhlope water-hole. This is a favourite drinking-place for both predators and antelope, as is the Manzimahle dam a few kilometres further south.

A third and often productive route from Skukuza is taking the H1-1 south for a few kilometres before turning left on to the S114. This road offers excellent game-viewing and the surrounding mixed combretum/acacia veld is my idea of true bushveld.

A wide variety of game can be seen in the area and there is a fair chance of spotting white rhino. I strongly recommend taking the S22 and visiting the Stevenson-Hamilton memorial, which offers a panoramic view and the chance to leave one's car.

Klipspringers and troops of baboons can often be seen on the rocky outcrops in the vicinity of the memorial and also on those a few kilometres to the south. Game is usually scattered about the Renosterkoppies dam.

If there is sufficient time, I recommend taking the S21 east and returning to Skukuza via the H4-1. The S21 offers a good chance of seeing white rhino and elephant cow herds.

A shorter return route would be to turn west along the S21, making one's way back to camp via the S65, S1 and H11. A diversion to the Granokop lookout point is recommended.

Pretoriuskop

Pretoriuskop is only nine kilometres from Numbi gate and is the third-largest camp in the park. The camp dates back to the 1870s, when it was on the route taken by transport riders as they carried supplies between Lourenço Marques and the eastern Transvaal goldfields.

With its well-kept lawns and shady trees, this camp has managed to retain much of the restful charm of the past. It has more than 140 thatched cottages and huts and a camp site with 60 sites. Other facilities include a small post office, a public telephone, a petrol station, a restaurant and a shop. A swimming-pool built into natural rock and surrounded by indigenous trees allows visitors to cool off on long, hot Lowveld days.

Pretoriuskop lies in a relatively high rainfall area and tall grass can make game-viewing difficult. The surrounding hilly countryside is dotted with attractive rocky outcrops and the dominant trees are silver cluster-leaf, sicklebush and marula.

Although this is not one of the park's better game-viewing areas, a large variety of animals, including the big five, can be found here. The most common species seen are kudu and impala, while wildebeest, zebra, giraffe, reedbuck, klipspringer and white rhino are regularly spotted. Keep an eye open for herds of roan, sable and eland and, possibly, even a black rhino.

The most popular game-viewing roads are the many loops in the vicinity of the camp. Numerous multicoloured granite outcrops beside these loops make fascinating subjects for photographers.

I recommend the short trip to the massive Shabeni rock formations, a few kilometres north-west of the camp. The S10 takes one up among these impressive formations and also provides good views of the surrounding countryside.

For visitors interested in history, the H2-2 follows the old transport road made famous by Sir Percy FitzPatrick in his book, *Jock of the Bushveld*. Impala and other antelope often graze at the foot of Ship Mountain, a prominent landmark beside the route.

There is another route from Pretoriuskop which is of historical interest. Take the S7 and S1 north and then turn west on to the S104 to the Albasini ruins. These are the remains of a trading-post established by João Albasini, the first white settler in the area.

Jock of the Bushveld

Jock of the Bushveld camp is near the confluence of the Mbyamiti and Mitomeni rivers and accommodates 12 people. This private camp is open only for block bookings.

Berg-en-dal

Mountainous scenery and modern facilities are the features of this camp. Built to help accommodate the increasing number of visitors to the park, Berg-en-dal was opened early in 1984. The nearest entrance gate to the camp is Malelane, some 12 kilometres to the south-west.

The thatched, face-brick buildings include over 90 huts and cottages, a restaurant and cafeteria, a shop, conference facilities and an information centre. Berg-en-dal has one of the best camp sites in the park. The more than 70 sites are on beautifully manicured lawns and provide good views of the surrounding mountains. The camp also boasts a swimming-pool and has a petrol station near its entrance gate.

Although a large variety of game occurs here including the big five, this is one of the park's less densely populated game areas. Visitors interested in birds, trees and scenery are likely to enjoy Berg-en-dal more than those interested only in animals.

Malelane

This small private camp was originally a lion-culling post. It accommodates up to 18 people and must be block-booked.

Crocodile Bridge

One of the smaller camps, Crocodile Bridge is in the extreme south east of the park. It has 23 huts and cottages and about 20 sites for camping.

Crocodile Bridge is ideally located for game drives on the H4-2, S28, S130 and S82. These routes are described in the section on Lower Sabie.

Lower Sabie

Overlooking the Sabie River and offering a variety of excellent game drives, Lower Sabie is one of the most popular camps in the park. It has over 80 huts and cottages, 30 camp sites, a restaurant, a petrol station and all the usual facilities. Large expanses of well-shaded lawns stretch down to the river and abundant birdlife adds to the attractions of this camp.

Virtually the entire area between Lower Sabie and Crocodile Bridge offers prime game-viewing. Although the bush gets dense in places, the general impression is one of flat, open plains dominated by acacia, red bushwillow, leadwood and marula. The thick grass cover is not dense enough to hinder game-viewing seriously.

For the first few kilometres southwards the H4-2 hugs the Sabie River and elephant and buffalo can usually be seen pushing their way through the reeds to drink. The road then enters the plains described above; these stretch to Crocodile

Bridge. Lion, cheetah, hyaena, buffalo, elephant, zebra, wildebeest, giraffe, warthog, kudu and impala are all seen regularly beside this road. The S82, S130 and S28 are equally good game-viewing roads, white rhino often being spotted to the west of the H4-2. Time spent at any of the water-holes in this area is likely to be rewarding.

A second productive route to take from Lower Sabie is westwards along the H4-1. The thick riverine vegetation and abundant wildlife beside this road are described in the section on Skukuza. On the way back to Lower Sabie, stop, I suggest, at the dam a short distance west of the camp. This is an excellent place for sunset photography and there are usually hippo, buffalo and water birds about.

For those wishing to journey further afield, Tshokwane is within easy reach of Lower Sabie. En route, be sure to stop and admire the magnificent views from the Mondolozi dam lookout point and from the various parking areas on the Nkumbe hill. The S29, S122 and H10 all offer fair game-viewing and a chance of seeing a zebra or a wildebeest migration. Look for klipspringer on the rocky outcrops on the Nkumbe hill.

Tshokwane

Just 40, 58 and 49 kilometres from Skukuza, Lower Sabie and Satara respectively, Tshokwane has no camp of its own. However, there are picnic sites at both the Eileen Orpen dam and the Tshokwane tea-room.

Although the vegetation to the west of the H1-3 is relatively dense combretum, the veld to the east is more open knobthorn/marula. All the common species of game are found here and include the big five. I highly recommend the circular route available on the S32, S35, H1-3 and H10.

It is worth spending some time at the Eileen Orpen dam. Good birdlife, a variety of animals and large crocodiles can usually be seen from the elevated lookout shelter. A pair of binoculars is recommended.

Some magnificent scenery can be viewed from Nkumbe lookout points a few kilometres to the south along the H10. Visitors can often look down on herds of elephant and buffalo, and klipspringer can be seen on the rocky outcrops.

Below: Sabie River sunrise. (H1-2 Skukuza)

Above: Hippo compete with each other to display their fearsome canines, which may be as long as seventy centimetres. Bulls are often seriously injured or even killed in territorial and dominance disputes. (Sabie River below Skukuza)

Below: Two delicate bushbuck does study the Sabie River for crocodiles before drinking. Although relatively shy antelope, they are often found in the vicinity of human settlements. This is probably because they do most of their browsing at night. (River below the Skukuza rest camp)

Right: Skukuza's thatched restaurant and tea-room complex has an old-world charm about it, and a balcony which overlooks the Sabie River.

Above: An impala doe stretches to reach some choice leaves while another grazes nearby. Impala are highly adaptable in their food requirements.

Above left: Giraffe are able to utilize a wide range of browsing which is out of reach to other animals.

Left: A pride of lions view some tourists with interest. It has been estimated that there are about 1 500 lions in the park, and most visitors place the big cats at the top of the list of animals they want to see. (S3 Skukuza)

Right: A massive pair of male lions at a kill. Males can weigh as much as 230 kilograms and stand one and a quarter metres at the shoulder. Note the size of the forearm and claws.

Above left: Mother's love. A lioness and her cubs.

Left: We found that Kruger Park lions were much more tolerant of black-backed jackals than of spotted hyaenas. The little carnivores were allowed to eat at kills immediately after the last lion had left the carcass. This gave them valuable time to bolt down food before hyaenas could approach and expropriate the remains.

Above: Early morning in the bushveld; a hyaena returns from a night's hunting, and a flock of helmeted guineafowl start their day's search for food. (S114 north of Renosterkoppies dam)

Above: A rainbow over Renosterkoppies. (S114 north of S21)

Left: A troop of baboons on one of the Renosterkoppie outcrops. At dusk, troops in this area often retire to boulders which are inaccessible to predators. Using fingertips and toes, they can climb almost vertical rockfaces. (S21 Renosterkoppies)

Right: The nimble klipspringer can bound up steep rockfaces with remarkable agility, and has adapted to rock-climbing by walking permanently on the tips of its hooves. When disturbed, the antelope makes for the heart of its rocky habitat, where it can easily outrun and outjump predators.

Above: Impala graze below Ship Mountain. In the old days the mountain was one of the major landmarks on the wagon trail from Delagoa Bay to the Escarpment. It was considered the western edge of the dreaded tsetse-fly belt. (H2-2)

Above: It is thought that the strikingly-coloured bateleur was given its name because of its love of performing antics while flying. The eagle occurs throughout the park, and flies great distances each day in its search for reptiles, small mammals, birds and carrion.

Below: The diminutive steenbuck weighs only seven to eight kilograms. They are normally solitary, except when mating or when the female has a lamb. Although preyed upon by most medium and larger mammalian predators, steenbuck are extremely agile and are rarely caught.

Above left: Lions catch a warthog. As the pigs have poor eyesight and often feed in open veld, they regularly fall prey to predators.

Left: Within minutes the warthog was ripped to pieces and eaten.

Right: Two square-lipped rhinoceroses. In spite of their formidable appearance, they are generally mild-natured animals. Virtually exterminated in South Africa by the turn of the last century, they were re-introduced into the Kruger Park in 1961. Their present population in the park totals more than 1 400.

Overleaf: The Shabeni rock formation, a few kilometres north-west of the Pretoriuskop rest camp, dominates the surrounding landscape.

Right: A family of warthogs. Warthogs sleep in the relative safety of underground burrows which the piglets enter headfirst. Adults always enter backwards so that their tusks are facing the entrance.

Above: The view looking towards the mountains of Malelane. (S110 Berg-en-dal)

Left: The rugged hill country of the Wolhuter wilderness trail area contains many attractive granite outcrops. The undulating plains at the foot of the hills are a favourite haunt of the square-lipped rhinoceros.

Right: Almost a hundred Bushman painting sites have been found in the park – many by game ranger Mike English. Most of the sites are in the southern section of the park, and are in shallow caves and rocky overhangs with views overlooking age-old game paths. To Mike, a dedicated conservationist, the greatest significance of paintings such as these is that they show what sort of animals used to occur in the region.

Below: The camp site at the Berg-en-dal rest camp.

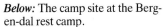

Left: A Cape glossy starling, its beak dusty with pollen, feeds on the nectar of an aloe. Various sunbirds, black-headed orioles and starlings feed on the nectar of the aloes found in most rest camps.

Right: Hippos may weigh as much as 2 000 kilograms, and eat up to 130 kilograms of grass a night. Their massive canines and incisors are useless for feeding and so they use their lips to pluck grass.

Below: The Sabie River shortly before it enters Moçambique.

Above: A lioness sharpens her claws on a tree-stump. In most instances claw-sharpening is an indication that hunting is about to begin.

Above right: When on a hunt, lions walk in a disciplined manner in rough single file.

Left: The African civet is mainly nocturnal and feeds on virtually any small creature, as well as wild fruit. It marks objects along the routes it travels with a secretion that retains its smell for as long as three months. This secretion was once used in the perfume trade and was known as civet.

Right: A lioness suffocates a blue wildebeest by cutting off the air supply through the mouth and nose, while the rest of the pride begin their feast.

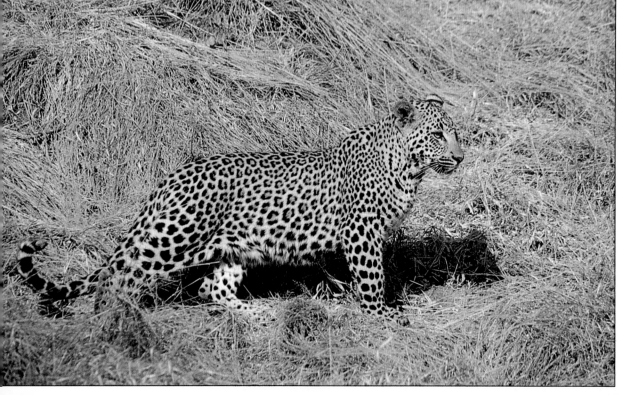

Above: Impala drink at a water-hole in the vicinity of the H4-1 in the Lower Sabie area. The thick bush of this area is one of the most densely populated impala areas in the park.

Right: A trio of graceful giraffe drink at a water-hole in the Lower Sabie area. Giraffe herds rarely consist of the same individuals for more than a few days.

Left: The leopard's black and golden rosettes blend in with virtually any habitat. Leopards can move much more silently than lions, and rely heavily on their stalking ability when hunting.

Left: The view eastwards from the Nkumbe lookout point, a few kilometres south of Tshokwane. This is an excellent place at which to spend a few peaceful hours and to see klipspringer. (H10 south of Tshokwane)

Above: Kruger elephants are renowned for their large tusks and this Tshokwane tusker was no exception. In much of Africa the ivory trade has resulted in the extermination of elephants carrying large ivory, leaving only small tuskers to breed. (S35 Tshokwane)

Right: Some entertaining baboon behaviour can be seen beside the Sabie River, as troops sun themselves in the early mornings. (H4-1 Skukuza)

Left: A lioness and a gathering of cubs and subadults cock their ears and listen. Although all their senses are well developed, lions detect most of their prey by listening.

Below: We witnessed thirty-five wildebeest kills during our nightwork in the Kruger Park. Once caught, the ungulates would immediately collapse without putting up a fight.

Above: A moment of pure magic for us as lions interrupt the hunt to drink at a rainwater pool.

Below: A small spotted genet curls up comfortably in a tree. Genets are nocturnal and, when disturbed, usually take to the trees until danger has passed. They feed on small mammals, rodents, insects and birds.

The Southern Central District

Satara

Nwanetsi

Orpen

Roodewal

PUNDA MARIA

SHINGWEDZI

LETABA

OLIFANTS
BALULE
ROODEWAL

SATARA
ORPEN
NWANETSI

TSHOKWANE

SKUKUZA

PRETORIUSKOP   LOWER SABIE

JOCK OF THE
BUSHVELD   CROCODILE BRIDGE
BERG-EN-DAL

MALELANE

0   25   50
Kilometres

Left: The popular Satara rest camp, surrounded by winter browns.

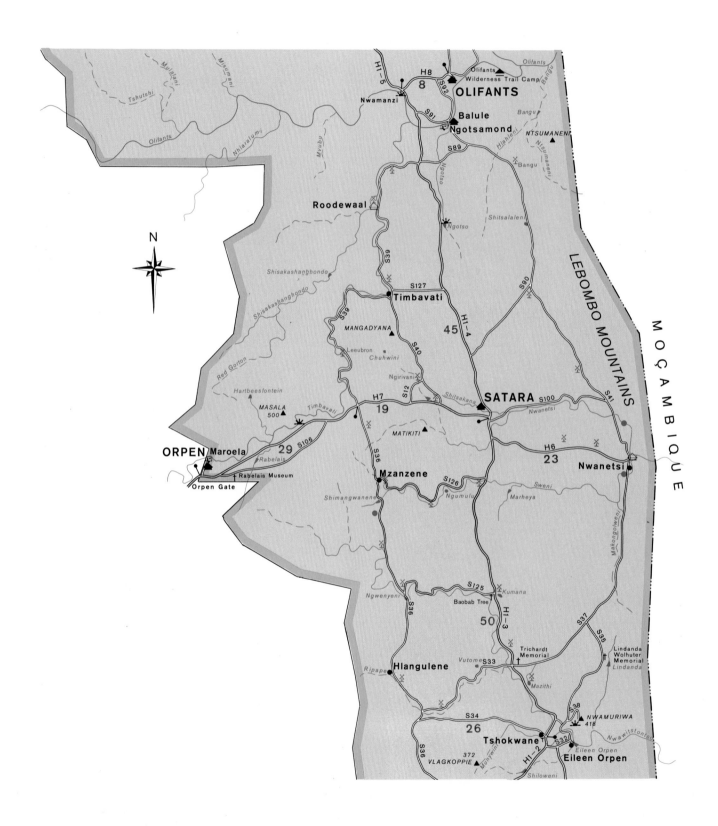

Satara

In extensive, rolling plains which stretch from Tshokwane to the Olifants River, Satara is the second-largest camp. It is usually heavily booked and is considered to be in one of the park's best lion areas.

The camp has more than 160 huts and cottages, and a large camp site with over 65 sites. There are the usual facilities as well as a self-service restaurant, a snack bar, a long, covered veranda, a coin-operated launderette, a shop, an AA office and a petrol station. There is excellent bird-watching in the vicinity of the veranda.

Satara's open grassy plains are dominated by knobthorn and, to a lesser extent, marula. Lion, leopard, cheetah, hyaena, zebra, wildebeest, waterbuck, kudu, impala, ostrich, elephant, warthog, giraffe and buffalo are all seen regularly.

Most of the roads in the Satara, Nwanetsi and Orpen areas provide good game-viewing. An excellent round trip is: take the S100 eastwards, then turn south along the S41 and visit the Nwanetsi picnic site, which has superb views of the Sweni River and the surrounding countryside. From the picnic site, go southwards on the S37, where concentrations of wildebeest and zebra can usually be seen during the summer months. After seven or eight kilometres, backtrack and take the H6 westwards before returning to camp on the H1-3. The S100 is one of the best roads in the park and the H6 can be almost as good. Both roads are renowned for predator sightings.

The H1-3 between Satara and Tshokwane is another fine road for seeing general game and predators. There are often herds of buffalo at the Kumana dam, which is also known for its large prides of lion. Time spent in the Tshokwane area usually proves worthwhile, and I recommend either backtracking on the H1-3, or returning to camp via the S37, S41 and S100.

Westwards on the H7 is another route. There are usually waterbuck, impala, zebra, warthog and wildebeest in the section close to the camp, and, as one travels westwards, the chances of seeing elephant cow herds increase. After the junction of the H7 and S39, continuing towards Orpen or taking the S39 northwards are equally productive routes. The S39 is particularly popular during the drier winter months, when animals congregate round the remaining pools in the Timbavati River or at the Leeubron water-hole. If returning to camp via the S40, visit the Ngirivani water-hole on the S12. This busy drinking-place is within easy reach of Satara.

Right: The colourful lilacbreasted roller is often known as Mosilikatze's roller, as the powerful Matabele king reserved the bird's beautiful feathers for his own use.

Nwanetsi

This popular private camp is on the banks of a river, and only a short distance from the rugged foothills of the Lebombo Mountains. The camp has accommodation for up to 15 people and must be block-booked.

Orpen

At the Orpen entrance gate, 46 kilometres west of Satara, this is a small camp with considerable charm. There is accommodation for 26 people and a reception office is in the small shop opposite the petrol station. Although there is no restaurant, a communal cooking-block has been provided. The well-shaded camp looks out over flat knobthorn/ marula veld.

Campers must stay at the Maroela camp site, two kilometres to the north, and check in at Orpen reception. This attractive camp site is in typical bushveld.

Orpen is an exceptionally good cheetah and lion area. There are not many roads but all are equally rewarding. Concentrations of game can usually be found at the Rabelais dam.

Roodewal

This is a private camp on the banks of the Timbavati River. It can accommodate up to 19 people and must be block-booked.

Above: A lappetfaced vulture holds out its wings to emphasize its size and intimidate several smaller whitebacked vultures. Often referred to as the 'king vulture', it is the largest of the species and is at the top of the pecking order at kills.

Left: A pride of lion at a waterbuck kill in the typical knobthorn/marula veld of Satara. The area is renowned for the density of its lion population.

Below: Unwilling to lose its position of dominance at the carcass, a lappetfaced vulture kicks out at a new arrival.

Right: A female ostrich holds up her wings captivatingly in the cutest of mating displays, which has the attention of the black and white feathered male. Normally monogamous, several females do sometimes accompany a male. (H1-4 north of Satara)

Below: On coming across this male ostrich, we did not realize he was incubating eggs until he stood up and moved off.

Left and right: The nest was just a bare patch of ground, and contained four eggs and two newly hatched chicks. A little beak was poking out of one of the eggs, but we decided against staying to watch the chick hatch in case this upset the male.

Far right: Although the chicks were still too weak to walk, their outsize legs were already prominent. Adult ostriches are able to run at about seventy kilometres an hour.

Sunset, and lions drink at a still pool.

Right: Lioness and cubs at the remains of a giraffe kill. Lionesses usually have litters of two or three cubs, although as many as six have been recorded.

Left: A furious male lion snarls his displeasure at the insubordinate behaviour of cubs at a kill.

Below: A prickly problem – how to tackle a porcupine? In the end these subadult lions conceded defeat and let the little animal go on its way.

Right: Unmistakable because of its luminously coloured beak, the saddlebill stork is found throughout the park, usually in the vicinity of water. The female has a yellow eye-ring, and the male a brown eye-ring and yellow wattle.

Left: The Nwanetsi lookout point is situated on a hill overlooking an attractive pool in the Sweni River. Visitors can sit in a comfortable thatched shelter and scan the surrounding countryside for wildlife and birds. (Junction of S37 and H6)

Below left: A herd of wildebeest in the lush summer grazing of Nwanetsi. When working with a lion pride in this area, we found that wildebeest comprised 61% of their prey.

Below: An elegant kudu cow, for many the most beautiful of all antelope.

A herd of waterbuck with two young males in the foreground. Predation among calves is high, as they are left alone in hiding-places for the first few weeks of their lives.

Nwanetsi lies in the summer grazing-grounds of a large zebra population which migrates northwards from the Sabie River. A zebra herd consists of a number of family groups, each with its own stallion, one or more mares, and their foals. There are also bachelor groups within the herd. (S37 Nwanetsi)

Right: Lions vie with each other for a place at a kill. Large prides like this often cover a carcass entirely, and look much like a rugby scrum with the ball hidden in the middle.

Left: Vultures retire to a tree for the night – a scene as old as Africa.

Below: Demonstrating superb team-work, a pride of lions attacks a buffalo bull. Buffalo are extremely dangerous prey, and quite capable of killing any lion careless enough to get within reach of their massive horns.

Above: After a night of feeding, buffalo come down to a dam in the Orpen area. They usually drink in the early mornings and in the late afternoons, and very often at the same place for consecutive days before moving off to another section of their home range.

Left: The snow-white plumage and yellow bill of a yellowbilled egret stand out against an African sky. The bird is usually found in the vicinity of vleis and rivers, where it feeds on frogs, fish and other aquatic life.

Right: There is a well-defined hierarchy among buffalo-herd bulls. This is established mainly by threat displays and during mock fighting. In these fights, bulls test each other's strength by locking horns and trying to push each other backwards.

The Northern Central District

Olifants

Letaba

Boulders

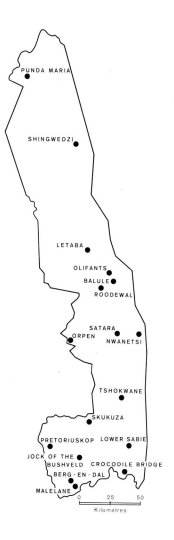

PUNDA MARIA

SHINGWEDZI

LETABA

OLIFANTS
BALULE
ROODEWAL

SATARA
ORPEN
NWANETSI

TSHOKWANE

SKUKUZA

PRETORIUSKOP LOWER SABIE

JOCK OF THE
BUSHVELD CROCODILE BRIDGE
BERG - EN - DAL
MALELANE

0   25   50
Kilometres

Left: Built on a hill overlooking an attractive section of the Olifants
River, the Olifants rest camp offers superb views.

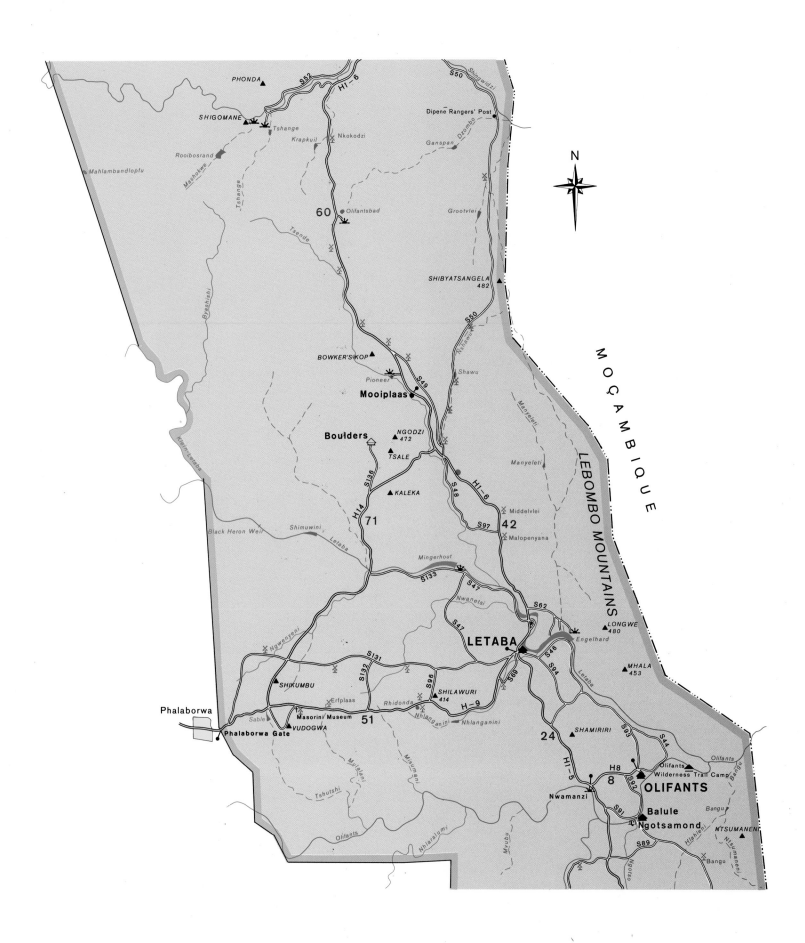

PHONDA ▲
S52
H1-6
S50 Shingwidzi

SHIGOMANE
Tshange
Krapkuil
Nkokodzi
Dipene Rangers' Post

Rooibosrand
Mashokwe
Mahlambandlopfu
Ganspan
Dzombo

Tshange
60
Olifantsbad
Grootvlei

Tsende
SHIBYATSANGELA
482

Bvashishi
S50
Nshawu

BOWKER'S KOP ▲
Shawu

Pioneer
S49
Manyeleti

Mooiplaas
Boulders
NGODZI ▲
472
Manyeleti

Klein Letaba
TSALE ▲
S136
H1-6

S48
KALEKA ▲
S97
42
Middelvlei

H14
71
Malopenyana

Black Heron Weir
Shimuwini
Letaba
Mingerhout
S133
S47
LONGWE ▲
480

Nwanetsi
S62
Engelhard

Ngwenyeni
LETABA
S46
MHALA ▲
453

S131
S132
S96
S69
S94

SHIKUMBU ▲
Erfplaas
Rhidonda
SHILAWURI ▲
414
H-9

Phalaborwa
Masorini Museum
51
Nhlanganini
Nhlanganini
24
SHAMIRIRI ▲
S93
S44
Olifants

Sable
VUDOGWA ▲
H1-5
H8
Olifants
Wilderness Trail Camp
Bangu

Phalaborwa Gate
Misumani
8
S92
OLIFANTS

Tshutshi
Nwamanzi
Balule
Bangu

Olifants
Nhlaralumi
S91
Ngotsamond
NTSUMANENI ▲

Mluvubu
S89
Hlahleni
Ngotso
Nisumaneni
Bangu

MOÇAMBIQUE

LEBOMBO MOUNTAINS

N

Olifants

There are few camps in any game reserve with views as magnificent as those of Olifants. Built on the edge of a high cliff, the camp looks down over one of the most beautiful sections of the Olifants River. It has 110 huts and cottages, and a small camp site with 15 sites. There is a reception office, a shop, a petrol station, a restaurant, a lounge where snacks are served, and a lookout shelter. Like many visitors, I am always entranced by the view from the lookout shelter. Cow herds of elephant often come down to drink immediately below the camp and there are usually buffalo, hippo and crocodiles in the pools and reeds.

The Nwamanzi lookout point on the H1-5 west of the camp also has superb views of the Olifants River. Visitors may leave their cars but must remain in the demarcated parking area.

Olifants is ideally situated for game-viewing, as it lies in the transition zone between the grassy plains to the south and the mopane-dominated veld to the north.

One of the advantages of staying at Olifants is that there is plenty of game close to the camp. The most common animals are kudu, impala, waterbuck, giraffe, buffalo and elephant. This is one of the better leopard areas and lion and hyaena are seen regularly.

The circular route (S92, S91, H1-5 and H8) is almost always productive. The loops off the S92 take one right down to the river and are excellent places at which to sit and wait for animals coming down to drink. There is abundant bird-life at this section of the river and elephant and buffalo can usually be seen in the reeds on the river bed.

There are several worthwhile diversions off this circular route. Take, for instance, the S90 southwards as far as the Bangu water-hole. A wide variety of animals drink here, especially during the drier months. Shortly after crossing the bridge, visitors can see a large Iron Age archaeological site which will become a feature of the new Ngotsamond caravan camp. This camp will replace Balule.

There is another popular diversion off the circular route: continue northwards along the H1-5 for a few kilometres and look for klipspringer on the Shamiriri rocky outcrops. En route the road passes one of the most attractive stretches of river in the park and loop roads take one right down to it.

It is worth stopping on the bridges of the H1-4 and S90. Both provide good bird-watching and excellent views up and down the Olifants River. Apart from numerous water birds and occasional hippo and crocodile, elephant and buffalo can often be seen from these bridges.

All the roads in the Letaba area are within easy reach of visitors staying at Olifants, as are the grassy plains to the south. Good views of the Letaba River may be had from the S44 and S93.

Letaba

Approximately 30 kilometres north of the Olifants River, Letaba lies well within the mopane-dominated veld which characterizes the northern section of the park.

Renowned for its tall, shady trees and views of the wide, sandy Letaba River, this medium-sized camp is a firm favourite with many visitors, especially those interested in elephant. It has over 90 huts and cottages and 30 sites for camping and caravanning. All the usual facilities include a coin-operated launderette and a veranda overlooking the river. I have spent many pleasant hours sipping refreshments on the veranda and watching elephant, impala, zebra, buffalo, giraffe and baboons coming down to drink.

My first impression of the expanse of mopane veld which surrounds Letaba was that it was an ideal habitat for elephant and perhaps buffalo, but not much else. However, I soon found that the mopane is home to a large number and variety of animals. Apart from elephant and buffalo, all the common species of antelope are present, as well as sable, roan, eland and tsessebe. There are many hyaena in the area and lion and leopard are often seen.

For those wishing to see breeding herds of elephant, I recommend driving very slowly along the H9 as far as the Winklehaak dam (Nhlanganini dam). Most of the herds approach from the north and have to cross the road before drinking. During the drier months, herd after herd of elephant often drink at the dam, and with them there is a good selection of other animals. There are always water birds about, as well as hippo and occasional crocodiles.

A very popular route is the drive northwards on the H1-6. This road hugs the river for the first few kilometres and animals must cross it to drink. Elephant, buffalo, giraffe, zebra, kudu, impala and troops of baboons are all likely to be here.

On approaching the bridge which spans the Letaba River, equally good routes are available: proceed northwards or take the S47 westwards. Tall trees, thick riverine vegetation and, occasionally, a good view of the river are characteristic of the S47. This can be an excellent road for seeing elephant as well as bushbuck and other animals common to Letaba. Continue to the Mingerhout dam and look for crocodiles sunning themselves beside the pool below the dam wall. Then backtrack to the H1-6 and continue northwards as far as the Middelvlei water-hole.

The H1-6 north of the bridge is one of the best stretches of road in the park. Apart from elephant bulls and the common game species, lions are often seen, as are rare tsessebe and roan. Large herds of buffalo drink at the Malopanyana water-hole, and concentrations of wildebeest and zebra gather at Middelvlei during the drier months. Hyaenas often use the road culverts in this area as dens.

There is a short route which is particularly good for elephant bulls: turn on to the S94 after leaving camp and then continue on the S46 to the Engelhard dam. Look for bushbuck on the section of the road opposite the camp. As you proceed, drive with extreme care. The mopane becomes tall and dense and elephant can often be seen only at the last moment as they step on to the road. There is usually good birdlife at the dam, as well as hippo, crocodiles and a variety of game.

A long but worthwhile drive from Letaba and a must for people entering or leaving the park through the Phalaborwa gate is a visit to the reconstructed Masorini village and its surroundings. Although much of the road between Letaba and Phalaborwa is uninteresting mopane scrub, there is a good chance of seeing sable, roan and even eland. The Erfplaas water-hole near Masorini is renowned for sable and, in the early mornings and late afternoons, large numbers of dassies sun themselves on the rocky outcrops to the east of this water-hole.

In my opinion even those who are not interested in history will enjoy visiting Masorini. There is a picnic site and a small museum, and a guide takes visitors on a tour of the village. Masorini's history dates back to the Stone Age and continues to more recent times, when its inhabitants made their living by forging iron implements. The village is built on the slopes of a steep hill and has magnificent views of the surrounding countryside.

There are numerous klipspringer at Masorini and on the rocky outcrops that line the S52 just west of the site. Visitors should continue on the S52 to the Sable dam, where I have seen lion, large herds of buffalo, sable and a wide variety of birds.

Boulders

This is a private camp and must be block-booked. It is southwest of Mooiplaas and has accommodation for up to 12 people.

Right: An attractive section of the Olifants River a few kilometres before its junction with the Timbavati River.

Right: The lookout shelter in the Olifants rest camp offers excellent game-viewing. Visitors can look down on elephant and buffalo or study crocodiles and hippo. Waterbuck, giraffe, kudu and impala can also usually be seen.

Left: In places along the Olifants Gorge, the rocks are interrupted by sandy beaches bearing the evidence of many journeys to the river to drink.

Below: The crocodile's skin maintains its beautifully rich colours for only a moment after leaving the water. Despite its short legs, the reptile is deceptively quick over short distances on land.

Right: We were impressed by the size of the many large crocodiles we saw in the Olifants River.

Below: An enormous hippo bull ponders over the body of another hippo. We wondered – was this a dead mate, or could he have killed the hippo in a territorial fight?

Below, middle and right: It took numerous crocodiles several days to devour the hippo. This was because they only managed to open up the tough hide in the soft spot below the tail. The reptiles entered the ever-growing cavity one at a time, took a mouthful of meat, and then twisted like a corkscrew to break the meat loose. They then backed out of the cavity and gulped down the meat.

Previous page: Giraffe silhouetted against the sunset.

Right: We followed this secretary bird for some time as it strode through the veld pouncing on and killing most of its victims with its feet. Once dead, even rodents were swallowed whole in one swift gulp.

Left: Two cheetah stand on a fallen tree-trunk to obtain an elevated view of the surrounding countryside and to look for prey. Estimates of their speed vary from 70 to 115 kilometres per hour.

Below: Although generally a peaceful animal, the honey badger's long knife-like claws and formidable teeth make it a dangerous adversary when roused. Its tough, loose skin is covered with heavy guard hair, and is virtually impenetrable to the bites of larger carnivores and to bee-stings. Even lions tend to leave honey badgers alone.

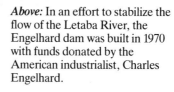

Above: In an effort to stabilize the flow of the Letaba River, the Engelhard dam was built in 1970 with funds donated by the American industrialist, Charles Engelhard.

Right: The well-shaded Letaba rest camp. A variety of animals, especially elephant and buffalo bulls, can be seen drinking in the river-bed below the rest camp.

Left: The attractive blister beetle (*Mylabris* sp) has no natural foes as its body contains cantharadin, which is poisonous. Cantharadin causes blisters if placed on the skin, and also has a reputation as an aphrodisiac. Spanish fly, *Lytta vesicatoria,* belongs to the same family of beetles.

Left: The Letaba River winds its way southwards through an expanse of winter-brown mopane towards its junction with the Olifants River.

Right: The view northwards from the Letaba rest camp, with the H1-6 on the left. In recent years, the Letaba River has stopped flowing regularly as a result of increased water usage outside the park.

Above: In order to teach an upstart of a crocodile a lesson for not moving out of his way, a bull elephant squirts the reptile with water. Elephant bulls are generally not aggressive and appear to possess a keen sense of humour.

Left: There is much affection in elephant society. Touch to demonstrate affection is every bit as important to the large herbivores as it is to humans.

Right: After drinking, elephants usually make for the nearest mud bath, where they attempt to cover those especially itchy spots with soothing mud. It is probable that mud is beneficial to their hides and may help to control parasites. (H9 Nhlanganini dam)

Left: Spotted hyaenas in the Kruger Park regularly adopt road culverts as dens. Litters usually number between one and four cubs, and very often several litters may share the same den. Adults rarely enter dens, preferring to suckle their young in the open. Unlike lions, the young of spotted hyaenas suckle only from their own mothers.

Above: Cubs usually come out from their dens shortly before sunset and spend an hour or so playing. There will most probably be a few adults about at this time, and, when the adults go off on the night's hunt, the cubs normally return to the safety of the den.

Below: In spite of the ungainly appearance of adult spotted hyaenas, the cubs are most appealing.

A terrified zebra, ears back and
muscles straining in a moment that
will decide life or death.

Above: Zebra in an autumn sea of mopane. (H1-6 north of Letaba)

Left: When we approached this Kori bustard, his two female companions ran off and he ducked beneath a bush. We felt he was protecting eggs or chicks. Whenever we approached closely, the bird splayed out its neck feathers in much the same manner as he would during a courtship display.

Right: A large rock dassie community lives in the numerous rocky crevices found in the Masorini hillside. Dassies spend most of the day sunning themselves, and always post a sentry to warn them of danger. Their main predators are the larger birds of prey, pythons and caracal.

Left: Some of the huts are situated in idyllic settings with magnificent views over the surrounding countryside. Because of the atmosphere we found ourselves imagining what life must have been like in the village.

Below right: A reconstructed iron-smelting furnace. Bellows made of a leather bag and a hollow waterbuck horn were used for blowing air through the slats in the side of the furnace.

Below left: National Parks Board guide, George Kozo, with a waterbuck-horn bellows.

Below: Situated on a hill not far from the Phalaborwa gate, the Masorini Iron Age site has been expertly reconstructed from ruins comprising little more than a few stone walls. There is a National Parks Board guide in attendance to take visitors on a tour of this interesting site. (H 9 Phalaborwa)

Right: The women of the baPhalaborwa tribe were competent potters and an attractive collection of clay pots and serving dishes is on display. The pots were, for example, used for carrying water, drinking and cooking.

Top: A massive eland bull and cows. Bulls may weigh as much as 700 kilograms and have a shoulder height as high as the average man. Eland are highly adaptable where habitat is concerned. We found them in the open shrub mopane veld of Mooiplaas and Vlakteplaas, and also in the lushness of Pafuri.

Above: Young zebra stallions are normally evicted from families before reaching maturity. They then join bachelor groups and spend much time sparring in preparation for the defence of the family groups they will eventually lead.

Right: A herd of semi-airborne eland bound over a recently burnt section of veld. Eland, the largest of all the African antelope, are mainly browsers and can jump two-metre-high obstacles with ease.

Below: Zebra and wildebeest wait their turn to approach a waterhole in the Mooiplaas area.

The Northern District

Shingwedzi

Punda Maria

Pafuri

Left: Surrounded by mopane, the Shingwedzi rest camp is in the heart of elephant country.

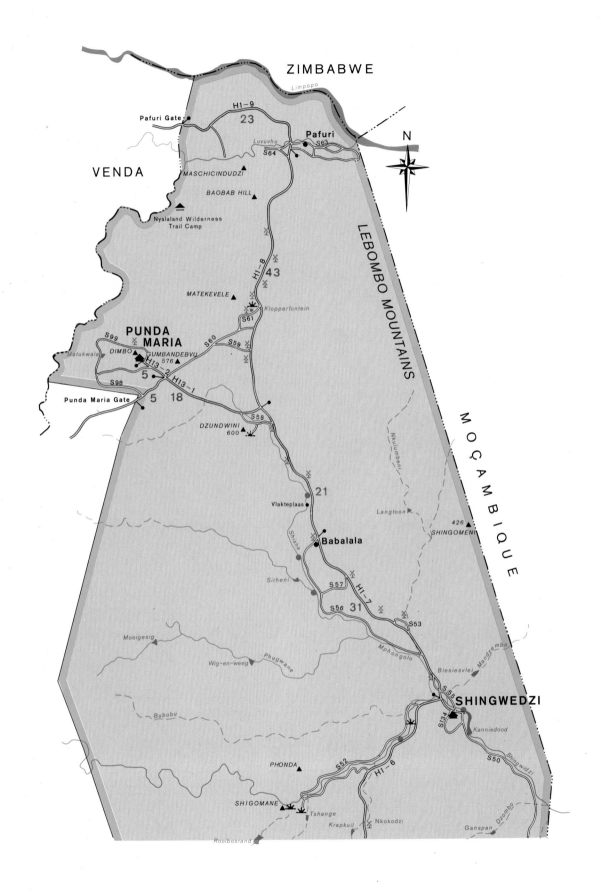

ZIMBABWE

Limpopo

Pafuri Gate

H1–9
23

Pafuri
S63

Luvuvhu

S64

VENDA

MASCHICINDUDZI ▲

BAOBAB HILL ▲

▲ Nyalaland Wilderness
Trail Camp

N

H1–8
43

MATEKEVELE ▲

Klopperfontein
S61

**PUNDA
MARIA**
S99

S60 S59

Matukwala
DIMBO ▲ GUMBANDEBVU
H13–2 576 ▲
5   H13–1

S98
5 18

Punda Maria Gate

S58
DZUNDWINI
600 ▲

LEBOMBO MOUNTAINS

Nkulumbeni

21

Vlakteplaas

Langtoon

426 ▲
SHINGOMENI

Shisha
☩ **Babalala**

Sirheni

S57
S56 31 H1–7

S53

Mphongolo

MOÇAMBIQUE

Mooigesig

Wig-en-weeg *Phugwane*

Biesiesvlei *Mandremba*

S55

Bububu

S134 **SHINGWEDZI**
▲
Kanniedood

PHONDA ▲

S52 H1–6 S50 *Shingwidzi*

SHIGOMANE ▲
Tshange

Krapkuil *Nkokodzi*

Ganspan *Dzombo*

Roolbosrand

136

Shingwedzi

The remoteness of Shingwedzi, which is more than 100 kilometres north of Letaba, has given it a special atmosphere. It is no wonder that this tranquil area is a haven for the big tuskers for which the Kruger is famous.

Built beside the Shingwidzi River, the camp has more than 80 huts and cottages, and 50 sites for camping and caravanning. The information centre, reception, shop, self-service cafeteria, restaurant and veranda are all in one large complex overlooking the river. Other features are an AA workshop, a petrol station and a swimming-pool. There is exceptionally good bird-watching in front of the veranda and round the camp site.

Although Shingwedzi is primarily known for elephant, the visitor will probably see a greater variety of game here than elsewhere in the park. All the common species are present and bushbuck, nyala, sable, tsessebe and roan are seen regularly. This is an excellent leopard area and there is abundant birdlife beside the river.

All the roads at Shingwedzi provide good game-viewing. One popular drive is southwards on the S50. There is no better place at which to look for big tuskers as they come down to drink. This is also a good road for impala, waterbuck, bushbuck, nyala and leopard. Numerous loops offer good views of the Kanniedood dam and its rich birdlife, which includes darters, herons, storks, kingfishers, duck and a large variety of other water birds. Continue, I suggest, on the S50 to the Dipene post, where the river turns east and enters Moçambique.

One of my favourite short drives is the road which joins the camp and the H1-6. There is plenty of game in this area and one can usually look down on herds of impala and waterbuck, or an occasional elephant or buffalo bull wandering along the wide, sandy river bed. This is a good section of river for water birds, and small crocodiles can be seen lying beside the pools.

A very popular route is the H1-7 northwards. The first 20 kilometres of this road are in prime elephant and buffalo country. As one proceeds, the mopane thins out and the chances of seeing tsessebe, roan and sable are good. Reedbuck can sometimes be spotted in the vicinity of the Babalala picnic site and eland further north.

I recommend a return to camp via the S56. Nyala, waterbuck, impala, bushbuck, kudu and baboons are all common near this road, which follows the Shisha and then the Mphongolo rivers. South of the junction of the Phugwane and the Mphongolo rivers the S56 is lined with tall, shady trees and can be one of the best roads in the park for seeing breeding herds of elephant. If they are in the area, they usually come down to drink from mid-morning onwards.

An alternative and often productive route is the H1-6 southwards as far as the Nkokodzi water-hole. A wide variety of game can be seen near this road, especially during the first few kilometres. Look for elephant drinking at an occasional pool beside the road. Returning on the H1-6, take the S52 to the Tshange lookout point. Visitors may leave their vehicles and enjoy spectacular views of the surrounding countryside. A pair of binoculars aids the spotting of game in the relatively open country below. All the species common to Shingwedzi may be seen beside the S52 loop.

Punda Maria

Built in 1934 on the lower slopes of a hill, this small camp still retains much of its 'Old Africa' charm. The surrounding area has one of the greatest varieties of plant species in the park and is renowned for its bird-watching. As the northern-most camp, Punda Maria also services the Pafuri region.

The camp's 23 huts are to be increased to over 50 and there are 48 sites for camping and caravanning. A small complex houses the shop, the reception and the restaurant and the petrol station is just inside the entrance gate. The camp site is my favourite because it offers the closest alternative to camping in the bush.

Punda lies in the park's highest rainfall area and is surrounded by luxuriant sandveld vegetation. During the summer months the thick bush and high grass cover can make game-viewing difficult but, once the area dries up, visibility improves considerably. Although one does not expect to see large numbers of animals here, there are all the common species, including the predators, and kudu, impala and nyala are quite common.

The S99 to the west of the camp provides some pleasant scenery and excellent bird-watching. During the drier months kudu, impala, nyala and, sometimes, shy eland can be seen at the water-holes beside the route.

To the east of the camp the gravel roads, S60, S59 and S61 can all be good game routes. Kudu are especially plentiful in the thick mopane and have a habit of jumping on to the road in front of vehicles, so drive slowly.

Pafuri

I am quite often asked which my favourite area in the Kruger is, and I have no hesitation in saying: 'Pafuri'. To me, this is the park's 'Garden of Eden'.

An hour and a half should be allowed for the drive from Punda to Pafuri. I suggest taking the S60 to the H1-8. As one drives northwards, baobabs become increasingly common and game can be seen occasionally. Eventually one tops the hill which overlooks the lushness of Pafuri. A few minutes later you are among some of the most spectacular riverine vegetation and forests you will see anywhere.

There are good views from the bridge across the Luvuvhu River. Then turn eastwards on the S63. Beside this road bushbuck and nyala are more plentiful than anywhere else in the park, and there are kudu, impala and baboons everywhere. Some of the more prominent trees are nyala, jackal berry, fever, sausage, sycamore fig, and Natal mahogany. Follow the S63 to the picnic site, which is next to the river. This is the sort of place where one can spend many hours soaking up the magic of the surroundings. The site is entirely shaded by a tall canopy of trees and the birdlife is so spectacular that bird-watchers often spend the entire day here.

From the picnic site continue eastwards and follow all the loops down to the river. This stretch of the Luvuvhu is the home of many crocodiles and it is quite usual to see 30 or more lying on a sandbank. Some of the loops take one close to the reptiles, which have become used to vehicles. Continue on the S63 as far as the turn-off to the police post, and then backtrack.

A second route is: turn west off the H1-8 on to the S64. As with the S63, this is an excellent road for nyala, bushbuck, kudu and impala. There are also quite a few baobabs.

Above: A herd of proud sable antelope. Their long sharp horns are used with lightning sweeps, and can become lethal weapons in territorial fights or in defence against predators.

Right: A territorial wildebeest bull attaches himself to a herd of fleet-footed tsessebe. Not known for their intelligence or alertness, wildebeest have been aptly named the clowns of the veld. Lone bulls often temporarily join up with more alert species in the hope of receiving an early warning of the approach of danger.

138

Above: Baobab sunset.

The leopard's expert tree-climbing ability enables it to store its kills in branches of trees which are inaccessible to other large predators. In this instance the impala lasted for three nights, the leopard eating twice nightly and resting elsewhere during the day. (S50 Kanniedood dam)

Above: Roan antelope race through typical shrub mopane veld to the east of the H1-7 at Vlakteplaas. Most of the park's ± 340 roan are found in the northern section and are annually inoculated against anthrax. Darts containing serum are fired into their rumps from a helicopter.

Above left: A breeding herd of elephant in typical mopane veld near Shingwedzi.

Left: Attractive red soils add a touch of colour to the countryside to the west of the H1-6.

Above: Precis natalica.

Left: The grey lourie or Go-away bird is well known to those who like to walk in the bushveld, and especially to hunters. The bird has the annoying habit of following humans about and uttering its 'go-away' call.

Right: With ears outspread to enhance his already enormous size, a bull elephant 'stands tall' in an effort to intimidate the photographer.

Below: Elephant herds are normally led by a wise old cow, who is much loved and relied on. There is a deep bond between herd members, and young elephants are cherished and spoilt by all.

144

Above: A plateau of baobabs (Nyalaland wilderness trail area).

Opposite top left: The gregarious wild dog lives and hunts in packs. They are most numerous in the southern district, but are often seen at Punda Maria.

Opposite top right: A male reedbuck in typical habitat. Reedbuck are grazers and usually live in pairs or family groups. Their most common habitat in the park is the tall grass and reeds next to marshes.

Left: The Punda Maria rest camp was built in 1933/34, and has maintained much of its 'Old Africa' charm. The surrounding area has one of the greatest varieties of plant species in the park and is also renowned for bird-watching.

Right: Portrait of a lioness.

Right: After leaving the Luvuvhu Gorge, the Luvuvhu River flows eastwards through one of the most remote and beautiful areas in the park.

Right: Flamingoes can sometimes be seen flying over the park, or resting at dams or pans. They seldom stay for long, as the Kruger Park does not have suitable water conditions for their feeding.

Left: Shortly before its junction with the Mutale River in the north-west of the park, the Luvuvhu River flows through the impressive Luvuvhu Gorge. In several places, elephants have made paths to the river below. We were astonished that the huge pachyderms could climb back up these precipitous paths.

Below: The high cliffs of the Lanner Gorge make ideal nesting sites for the Lanner falcon, after which the gorge is named. Another resident of the gorge is the black eagle, which preys mainly on dassies (rock hyrax).

Left: The early morning view from the bridge across the Luvuvhu River. (H1-8 Pafuri)

Below: Swainson's francolin, the only francolin in the park with a red face and neck.

Above: Three whitefronted bee-eaters proudly display their catch of insects before flying off to feed their young. The birds live in colonies, nesting in deep holes burrowed close together in river banks. (S63 Pafuri)

Above and left: The S63 at Pafuri winds its way through a variety of lush tropical scenery, and offers superb views of the Luvuvhu River.

Right: A nyala bull. Nyala are a gregarious species and are usually seen in small herds seldom numbering more than a dozen. Nyala are not territorial and herds are only of a temporary nature. (S63 Pafuri)

Below: Leopards are secretive animals and difficult to observe. Females usually have litters of two or three. Cubs are weaned when about three months of age, after which they accompany mothers on hunts and gradually learn to fend for themselves before becoming solitary.

Previous page: The magic of a sycamore fig-tree forest. High above the ground, the deep 'boom' and other loud vocalizations of re-introduced samango monkeys often echo through this forest as they feed on figs and nutritious leaves.

Left and right: A forest of fever trees, brilliantly aglow in the early morning sunlight. The trees are generally found in low-lying swampy areas, the favourite habitat of the malaria-carrying mosquito. Because of this, the early pioneers mistakenly thought the trees caused malaria, hence the name. (S63 Pafuri)

Below right: Kudu are plentiful at Pafuri. The best time to see them is in the early morning or late afternoon. (S63 Pafuri)

Below: An elegant kudu bull and cow in the tall grass beneath a fever-tree forest. Kudu are quite at home in the thickest bush. When disturbed, they utter loud, sharp barks and bound away in graceful leaps up to two metres high.

Left: An epauletted fruit bat and her young. The bats live in colonies of up to several hundred individuals, and spend their days hanging upside-down from the branches of heavily-shaded trees. At night they forage for figs, marulas, mobola plums, kudu berries and other wild fruit.

Far left: Vervet monkeys live in troops, with each individual having a clearly defined position in the order of dominance. They are mainly vegetarians and feed on a wide variety of fruits, flowers, seeds and pods. They also eat insects and birds' eggs.

Right: The fiercely territorial fish eagle, feathered king of the park's rivers and dams. The eagle preys mainly on fish, but also occasionally on other birds.

Left: The tall tropical forests which line the Luvuvhu River extend inland for almost a kilometre in places, and are a bird-watcher's paradise.

Below: Egyptian geese are by far the noisiest residents of Pafuri. Each family has its own stretch of river, which it jealously guards, and any intrusion is used as an excuse for their raucous honking and hissing.

Left: Joined by its tributary the Luvuvhu, a swiftly flowing Limpopo River races eastwards into Moçambique. Just beyond the junction of the two rivers the boundaries of Zimbabwe, Moçambique and the Kruger National Park meet. In the old days this densely forested area was known as 'Crook's Corner'.

Right: A nyala cow, one of the most beautiful and inquisitive of all antelope. Nyala are often found in the vicinity of baboons. The primates are excellent sentries and drop on the ground a lot of half-eaten fruit which the nyala eat with relish.

Below right: Nose held high to catch our scent, a buffalo inquisitively inspects our vehicle. Although they possess quite good eyesight, buffalo appear to be able to deduce more from smell than sight, as is the case with many animals.

Below: Hippo push their way up through the vegetation covering the surface of a pan deep within a Limpopo forest. At night the hippo leave the forest to graze in the surrounding flood-plains.

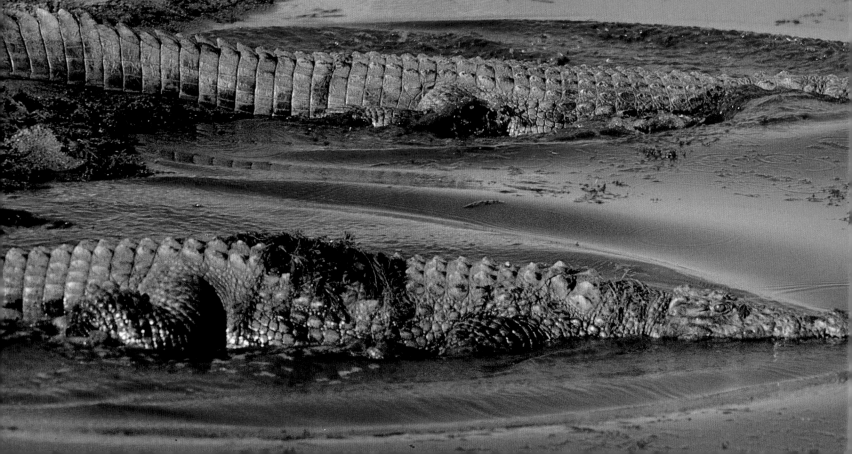

Above: The confluence of the Limpopo and Luvuvhu rivers – a favourite haunt of crocodiles.

Right: Although appearing impenetrably dense when viewed from above, the luxuriant forests which line the southern banks of the Limpopo River are easily accessible at ground level. The forests are alive with birdlife, and are traversed by a wide variety of game on their way to and from the Limpopo to drink.

Left: Two crocodiles slide quietly into the water. In spite of their sluggish appearance, they have acute hearing and eyesight, and are among the most difficult of all animals to approach without being detected.

Above: Situated midway between the Luvuvhu and the Limpopo River, this long, narrow pan is a favourite haunt of herds of buffalo, kudu and nyala. We were surprised to find large numbers of crocodiles in the pan, presumably feeding off the numerous barbel fish trapped in the shallow water. Once pans dry up, crocodiles have no trouble in walking a few kilometres overland to more permanent water.

Left: A mighty baobab, perhaps more than 3 000 years old. African folklore has it that when God became angry with the baobab, he threw it out of heaven and it landed with its roots in the air. Baobabs occur mainly in the northern part of the park.

Right: Just as humans are normally right- or left-handed, elephants usually use only one of their tusks for digging or for stripping bark or wood off tree-trunks. As a result of this, one tusk is normally shorter than the other. Quite often, tusks are broken off in this way.

Above: Sunset over the Limpopo
River.

APPENDIX

WILDLIFE PHOTOGRAPHY

Perhaps the most fascinating aspect of wildlife photography is that there is always so much to learn – about photography and about wildlife. This is probably why so many wildlife photographers tend to specialize.

Beginners should realize that there is no one best combination of equipment or best way of photographing each wildlife subject; it is all a matter of individual preference and experience.

Cameras

Several years ago, choosing a camera suitable for wildlife photography was relatively simple. Although there were many models, their features were not so very different. Today, even the most experienced professionals have difficulty in choosing; the various models offer a host of different features.

In my opinion the first question the beginner must ask is: 'Just how much photography will I be doing?' If the camera is to be used only on an occasional trip to a game reserve, an auto-everything model is probably best. This is because manual control requires many exposed rolls of film and, therefore, much time and effort to achieve a standard of exposure and focussing comparable to that immediately obtainable with today's sophisticated multi-program autofocus cameras.

On the other hand, if you want to become a serious photographer, you need to learn the technical side of photography so as to enjoy the creativity of making your own photographic decisions. To be able to do this a camera with manual focussing and exposure is needed.

At present there are basically two types of 35 mm cameras with manual focussing and exposure: those that have been primarily designed for this type of use and may or may not have program modes, and those that have been designed for programmed use but have provision for manual focussing and exposure. The former have traditional aperture and shutter speed set rings, and the latter are mainly push-button controlled. I rarely use program modes and prefer the former type of camera. However, I suggest trying both types in the shop before choosing. Compare how fast you can focus manually in poor light, and manually change speed and aperture settings. In wildlife photography, a split-second delay often costs you the photograph.

There are several other points to consider when buying a camera for wildlife photography.

The metering systems of most cameras provide centre-weighted averaging admirable for wildlife photography. Those cameras which also have spot metering offer an additional advantage as you will often be able to take direct readings off animals' coats and hides when using a long telephoto lens.

It is important to buy a camera with a focussing screen suitable for telephoto use. I suggest a matte/fresnel field with a clear matte centre spot. Many cameras are sold with split-image/microprism collar focussing screens, and in poor light conditions one half of the rangefinder often blacks out. This can be particularly frustrating when using a telephoto lens in the late afternoon. Fortunately, it is often possible to change the focussing screen.

Although motor-drives and power-winders are very useful for fast shooting, they make a good deal of noise. When you are working from a hide, or even photographing animals close to the car, this noise often scares them off. On the other hand, the sound of a motor-drive can be used to make animals look at the camera. In any event, one should make sure that, if a winder is built into the camera, it can be turned off and the film advanced manually.

Film

Using correct film is as important as choosing photographic equipment. Virtually all wildlife photography is done on colour-slide film.

Photographers who take photographs for publication need a very fine grain 35 mm film. Consequently, professional wildlife photographers usually use a 25, 50 or 64 ASA film. For most amateurs such a slow film is probably more of a hindrance than a help. It often means using telephoto lenses at very slow shutter speeds, and this encourages camera shake. For this reason, I recommend a 100 ASA film; it is fast enough to make reasonable shake control possible, and slow enough for quality results. Of course, as technology advances, we can expect finer and finer grained films.

When choosing brands of film, remember that no two films give the same results. Some have more colour saturation in certain colours and most have a noticeable colour bias. For instance, one popular slide film has a slight yellow/red bias. Its main rival has a slight cyan bias. If used in early morning light the former may produce unacceptably yellow results unless used with a cyan lens filter. The film with a slight cyan bias produces well-balanced early morning colours but, generally, colder results once the sun is high.

The best way to compare films is to test them yourself. If you have two cameras this makes matters much easier, as films should be tested under the same lighting conditions and on the same subjects. Normally I test films outdoors and on subjects with colours similar to those of wildlife photography. Once you have found a film which you like, get to know all about it: what sort of results it gives you on cloudy days and in all light conditions; how well it brings out shadow detail; and how much exposure latitude it has.

The importance of good film processing cannot be overstressed. It is heartbreaking to spend a great deal of time, money and effort securing good photographs only to have them ruined by poor processing. I once spent a month in Botswana photographing with a well-known British photographer. After the trip, he had several hundreds of rolls of film processed by two of Johannesburg's leading processing laboratories. The one lot of film was well processed with beautifully rich colours and lots of sparkle. The other was a complete write-off – dull colours and lots of water-marks and scratches. In my experience it is very difficult to find good film processing. But it is essential.

Lenses

Many beginners buy expensive cameras which have a host of features they will never use, and cheap lenses. This is wrong. After all, it is not the camera but the optical quality of the lens which primarily determines the sharpness, contrast and colour rendition of the pictures you will take. It is much better to buy a camera which has only the features you will need, and to spend the money saved on better lenses.

Let us assume that most of your wildlife photography will be done from a vehicle. Short and medium telephoto lenses will be needed for photographing herds, scenics, and large animals close to the vehicle, and a long telephoto lens for subjects further away and for bird photography.

Some years ago the professional wildlife photographer's short and medium telephoto lens selection probably included 80 mm, 135 mm and 200 mm lenses. But, as the optical quality of today's short to medium telephoto zooms is often equivalent to their single focal length counterparts, the 70-210 mm and 80-200 mm zooms have become very popular. Not only do these zooms allow the photographer to carry one lens instead of three, but they are compact, easy to use and allow exact framing of pictures.

An alternative to these zooms is the 100-300 mm lens. For me, its drawback is that it does not include the short telephoto lens. This means delays for unnecessary lens changes. I also find that when I need a magnification of more than 200 mm, I usually require at least a 400 mm lens.

There are quality zooms which include all the focal lengths of the short and medium telephoto: for instance, the 50-300 F5.6 zooms. These are larger than the above-mentioned zooms and have to be used with the same care as the long telephoto lenses if camera shake is to be avoided. However, zooms are getting faster and more compact all the time.

One disadvantage of zooms covering the short to medium telephoto range is that they are one to two stops slower than the equivalent single focal length lens. This results in a dimmer image seen through the viewfinder and more difficult focussing. For instance, a 135 mm F2 lens snaps in and out of focus much more crisply than the 70-210 F4 zoom.

Deciding on a suitable long telephoto lens

is more straightforward. The common focal lengths in this category are 400 mm, 500 mm, 600 mm and 800 mm. The big advantage of the 400 mm lens is that it is compact enough to be easily manoeuvrable in a vehicle, while it can also be hand-held in good light conditions. It is the ideal lens for telephoto photography in most of our national parks. Lenses longer than 400 mm must be mounted on a sturdy tripod or rest, and are generally for specialized use such as bird photography or photographing animals at great distances in open habitat.

Photographing from a vehicle
When on a game drive, make sure your equipment is always ready for use and close at hand. If you see a leopard walking across the road, it is no use stopping the vehicle, reaching into the back for your equipment, selecting and mounting the correct lens, setting the shutter speed and aperture, and then, finally, being ready to focus and shoot. By this time, the animal will probably have disappeared.

To work quickly I always try to get someone else to drive. Ideally, your camera case should be on the seat next to you, the lenses most often used mounted, and the shutter speeds set. On seeing an animal ahead, all you have to do is to flip open the camera case, take out the appropriate lens/camera combination, set the aperture while the vehicle slows down, and, immediately on halting, focus and shoot. A rough guide for setting shutter speeds is that a 500 mm lens should be used at 1/500 sec or faster, a 250 mm lens at 1/250 sec, etc.

Useful additional equipment
There is no need to buy expensive aluminium camera cases. Any inexpensive suitcase with hard sides will do. Tightly pack both the lid and the bottom part of the suitcase with foam rubber and cut out a section for each piece of equipment so that it fits snugly into the foam and will not shift when the case is closed.

Although short and medium telephoto lenses, and even the 400 mm lens can be hand-held in suitable light conditions, it is best to use a support if there is sufficient time. There are various tripod attachments which mount on to car windows and doors. But I have always found that a simple cloth bean bag, draped over the open window, is the easiest and steadiest support to use. My bean bags are usually about 350 mm – 400 mm long, have a similar circumference, and contain either beans or rice.

A digital spot meter is invaluable for wildlife photography. One might come across a buffalo bull in dry grass. If the buffalo fills only a small part of the frame, the camera meter will probably expose for the grass, and the buffalo will be very underexposed. With the digital spot meter one can quickly take readings off the grass, the buffalo's coat, and any other subjects that need to be considered, and can then calculate the best exposure.

What this will be will depend on how you want each subject to look. For instance, the reading off the buffalo's coat could be 1/250 sec at F5.6, and the grass 1/250 sec at F16. One could settle for an exposure of 1/250 sec at F11; to underexpose a black subject such as a buffalo by more than one stop would result in too big a loss in detail. On the other hand, to overexpose dry grass by two stops can give a pleasant effect. To me this is what creativity and making one's own photographic decisions is all about.

If possible, you should buy a digital spot meter which also has attachments enabling flash and incident readings to be taken. Incident readings are useful in low-light conditions as in forests, and flash readings are valuable when you are doing macro photography.

Putting together a slide show
Most of us have had the experience of being invited to a slide show on a game reserve we have always wanted to visit, only to come away with no idea of what the area looks like. More often than not the entire presentation consists of hundreds of repetitive pictures of animals and nothing else.

Subjecting one's friends to this can easily be avoided with a little planning. This should start prior to the trip, and result in taking pictures with the slide show in mind. Having this additional incentive makes photography more interesting and enjoyable.

Putting together such a slide show is similar to making a documentary. It should be well-balanced, non-repetitive and ruthlessly trimmed. There should be plenty of scenic pictures of each area visited, and these should act as a base for the presentation. Pictures of animals should be slotted into the areas in which they were taken, and there should be interesting fill-ins of people, birds, reptiles, etc.

Wildlife pictures can be divided into categories such as portraits and behavioural and action shots. Wherever possible, preference should be given to the last two categories, as they have more viewer interest than 'that's a zebra standing there' type of picture. Where one has several good but similar shots of a particular animal doing something, use only one in order not to lose impact. The result will be a valuable record of a trip.

GAME-VIEWING

Many visitors to the park will not have been able to spend much time in the bush. I hope that this information will help them to enjoy more successful game-viewing.

An important and often neglected part of game-viewing is planning the trip. It is necessary to decide what you want to see and where to see it, and then to apportion the time to be spent in each area. For those unfamiliar with the park this means doing a good deal of homework. The result, however, will be a more productive and

enjoyable holiday. Much of the information required can be found in the preceding chapters.

The influence of food and water on game movements
In comparison with most parks, the Kruger is blessed with an abundance of water. There are seven major rivers and numerous streams, many of which hold water during the dry season. There are also windmill/water-holes and dams throughout the park. In spite of this, water plays an important part in most years in determining game movements and concentrations.

Generally, the first heavy rains fall in late August or in September, and fill numerous pans and pools. Within a short time the game disperses to take advantage of the lush summer grazing and browsing, especially that which was previously quite far from water. By March most of the rains have fallen and the pans start to dry up. By June nearly all the smaller pans are dry, and concentrations of game increase round the permanent water sources.

Advantages of the dry season
You are likely to see more game during the dry season as animals congregate in the vicinity of the water-holes. Also, the game is easier to spot as the grass and leaf cover is much less dense. There are fewer clouds to hinder photography and winter browns are the order of the day. One drawback of the dry season is that many of the park's neighbours burn their grass and the resultant haze can make scenic photography difficult.

Advantages of the wet season
This is a time of new life. The park is clothed in lush greens, the antelope drop their young, many of the birds display their breeding plumage, there is a wealth of interesting insect life, and migratory birds become resident once more. As there is water everywhere and the grass and leaf cover is very thick, one is likely to see less game. On the other hand, the animals one does see have shiny, dust-free coats. Clouds and rain can be a problem for photographers.

General game-viewing
Just as humans are fairly habitual as to when they sleep, eat and relax, so most animals follow some sort of routine. These routines vary from species to species and from season to season and tend to be disrupted during cold and windy weather. The more you can learn about these routines, the easier it is to organize your game-viewing. Just a few days of careful observation should enable you to anticipate the movements of the more common species. You can estimate, for instance, the time elephants are likely to start coming down to drink at a certain water-hole, or when a troop of baboons will sun themselves beside a road. Ask the camp's information officers about current game movements, as they get continual feedback

from visitors.

The best time to view animals is in the early morning or late afternoon. Once it starts getting hot, many of the animals retire to shade, perhaps emerging once during the heat of the day for a drink at a nearby water source. I usually finish my morning game drive by 8 am, and then either make my way back to camp or go and sit next to a water-hole.

Basically, there are two methods of game-viewing: spotting animals while you drive, or sitting at a selected spot such as a water-hole, and waiting for the game to come into sight.

Game drives
The usual speed limit in the park is 50 kilometres an hour on tarred roads and 40 kilometres an hour on sand roads. As much of the park has a relatively dense grass and bush cover, you will usually want to drive much more slowly than this. Generally, the thicker the bush, the more slowly one drives. When travelling through thick bush, do not look at the trees in the foreground; look between them as far into the background as you can. During the hotter hours, animals often lie or stand in the shadows.

The lush new grass which sprouts in recently burned areas usually attracts concentrations of antelope. These burned blocks of veld are particularly valuable for game-viewing in high-grass areas such as Pretoriuskop.

Water-holes
Before deciding to spend any time at a water-hole, check to see if it is well-used by animals. There is usually very little grass round busy water-holes and the surrounding trees are heavily browsed. Numerous well-worn game paths leading down to the water and plenty of fresh animal droppings and spoor are also good signs. It is not much use sitting at a water-hole for a few minutes and then driving off if nothing comes down to drink. Patience is needed and is usually rewarded.

While waiting for game to come down to drink, make a habit of checking the surroundings with binoculars. There is always good birdlife round water-holes: kingfishers and herons fishing, darters sunning themselves, and jacanas squabbling over territories. Many of the larger water-holes and dams harbour crocodiles and hippos, and terrapins can often be seen competing for positions on rocks and logs.

Predators
Although lions, leopards and hyaenas are occasionally active during the day, they do most of their hunting at night. They are all fond of sunning themselves in the early morning before retiring to a burrow or shady spot for the day. Lions often lie on roads at this time. So, if you want to see the larger predators, leave camp as soon as the gates open. An hour later is generally too late. Cheetahs and wild dogs are most active during the early mornings and late afternoons.

You can often spot predators by watching the movements of other animals. For instance, if there are hyaenas and jackals pacing impatiently backwards and forwards, they are probably waiting for lions to leave a kill. A large gathering of vultures in trees is often an indication of predators on a carcass.

If impala rams are standing still and continually staring in a particular direction, they may have spotted a predator. Wildebeest often snort continually at nearby lions; impala also do this.

Most predators, especially the cats, are opportunists. Even if resting, they often try to catch approaching prey. If you see lions at a water-hole, lying beside a game path or concealed in grass, it is worth watching them. These situations offer visitors the best chance of seeing a kill.

When looking for prey, cheetahs often stand on fallen trees to get a clear view over the grass. If you see them doing this, they are probably hunting.

Hyaenas milling about underneath a tree may be an indication that there is a leopard's kill in the tree. If you see such a kill, sit near it in the early mornings and late afternoons, as those are the times you are most likely to see the leopard feeding. An impala kill usually lasts a leopard about three days.

Birds
Good places to look for birds are at river crossings, dams, water-holes, picnic sites and the camps. In fact, the camps offer some of the finest bird-watching in the park. This is because the birds are used to humans and often congregate round the camp sites and cafeterias in the hope of scavenging and finding tasty morsels. You can usually get very close to the many sunbirds, orioles and starlings which feed off the nectar of the aloes found in most camps. Squirrels and lizards also become quite tame in the camps.

INFORMATION FOR VISITORS

Reservations
Reservations, tariffs and other information are obtainable from:
The Reservations Office
National Parks Board
PO Box 787
PRETORIA
0001
Telephone: 012-3431991

Climate
The park's rain falls mainly in the summer, when the days are usually hot and the nights are warm. During winter the days are often pleasantly warm, but the nights and early mornings can get very cold. The average daily maximum temperature is 30°C (January) and the minimum is 8°C (July).

Clothing
Wear casual clothes. Warm clothes are essential in winter and, occasionally, are needed in summer.

Health precautions
The Kruger National Park is in a malaria area and anti-malaria tablets must be taken.

Accommodation
Huts, cottages and rondavels are available and are supplied with beds, bedding, towels and soap. Most have air-conditioning or fans, and electric lights. Those with bathrooms or showers have hot and cold running water, while those without have basins with cold water. Many cottages and rondavels without kitchenettes have refrigerators. Those with kitchenettes have cooking utensils, crockery, cutlery, glassware, gas stoves and refrigerators. Outdoor cooking facilities are available at all camps, but visitors must supply their own utensils.

The camps are not floodlit, and a torch is essential.

The camp sites have outdoor cooking facilities and ablution blocks with hot and cold running water. Campers must bring their own camping equipment, cooking and eating utensils, bedding and towels.

Accommodation especially designed for paraplegics is available at Skukuza, Satara, Shingwedzi, Berg-en-dal, Olifants, Letaba and Lower Sabie.

Shops, restaurants and cafeterias
Shops are stocked with basic groceries, tinned foods, frozen meat, vegetables, bread, dairy produce, cool drinks, liquor, cooking and eating utensils, gas, film, curios, books, postcards and a limited range of clothing.

Restaurants are open for breakfast, lunch and dinner, while the cafeterias are open throughout the day and sell snacks, cool drinks, tea and coffee.

Laundry
Facilities for washing clothes are available throughout the park, and there are coin-operated laundromats at many of the larger camps.

Fuel and motor repairs
Petrol, oil and diesel are available at all the major camps.

The AA has emergency service centres at Skukuza and Letaba, where minor repairs are done and where spare parts, tyres and batteries are sold. The AA also operates various patrol and tow-in services.

Day visitors
Day visitors must obtain permits if planning to visit the park during a long weekend, school holiday or public holiday.

Payments
All payments must be made in cash, by traveller's cheque or by credit card. Fuel must be paid for in cash, by bank-guaranteed petrol cheques or petrol card.

There is a Volkskas bank and Multi-net automatic teller at Skukuza.

APPENDIX

General

There are daily flights to Skukuza from Johannesburg and Phalaborwa. Cars can be hired at Skukuza.

Mail can be posted at all reception offices and there is a post office at Skukuza.

Various tours of the park are provided by SATOUR and other outside organizations.

Regulations

1. Stay in your vehicle, keep to the road, and pay attention to the traffic signs.
2. The general speed limit in the park is 50 km/h on the tarred roads and 40 km/h on dirt roads. Do not exceed the speed limit and do not allow anyone without a valid driver's licence to drive.
3. Do not feed or disturb the animals and do not damage or remove plants.
4. Do not discard cigarette ends, etc; prevent veld fires.
5. No pets are allowed in the park.
6. Keep your park clean.
7. You must spend the nights in a rest camp and you must report your presence to the management.
8. Do not disturb others, especially from 21h00 to 06h00.
9. You may not advertise or offer any goods for sale or entertain the public for remuneration.
10. No roller skates or bicycles are allowed in rest camps.
11. No generators are to be used between sunset and sunrise.
12. Firearms must be handed over to be sealed at the entrance gates.

Acknowledgements

It would not have been possible to produce this book without the assistance
and encouragement of many people and organisations.
To everyone who assisted me, I extend my sincerest thanks.

My very special thanks to:
The National Parks Board and the then Warden of the Kruger National Park,
Dr U de V Pienaar, for granting me the privilege of photographing in this famous national park.

Debbie Fair for her dedication throughout the project.
I could not have wished for a more capable assistant or a better companion.

Johan Kloppers, Head of Wildlife Management in the Kruger National Park,
who made many things possible and who interrupted a very busy schedule to grant
the interview on wildlife management.

David Chapman for the interview on wilderness trails.

Hugo van Niekerk, chief pilot of the National Parks Board,
whose expert flying made aerial photography a pleasure.

Bruce Bryden, chief ranger of the Kruger National Park, for organising this project.

The following game rangers for their kindness, assistance and advice:
Kobus Botha, Mike English, Ampie Espag, Leighton Hare, Andrew Hofmeyer, Kobus Kruger,
Ben Lamprecht, the late Thys Mostert, Flip Nel, Louis Olivier, Ben Pretorius, Johan Steyn,
Swanni Swanepoel, Dirk Swart, Johan van Graan, Lynn van Rooyen, Pete van Staden,
Ludwig Wagener, Ted Whitfield, Pat Wolff and Tom Yssel.

Dr U de V Pienaar, Dr S Joubert, Johan Kloppers, Joanita Fourie and Rufus Coleman for
meticulously checking the manuscript and offering many valuable suggestions and corrections.

Peter Palm, Irene Grobler, Graham Cox, Leo Braack and Annetjie Moll.

Joan Wolhuter for allowing me to quote from 'Memories of a Game Ranger.'
J C Stevenson-Hamilton for allowing me to quote from his late father's works.

Production acknowledgements

Cover design: Jeremy Woodhouse
Language consultant: Professor A Lennox-Short
Maps: Helena Margeot and Raymond Poonsamy
Proof reader and indexer: Debbie Fair
Reproduction: Hirt & Carter, Natal
Typesetting: Chris Uniacke of Positone, Pinetown

Index

INDEX